EVALUATIVE INQUIRY

EVALUATIVE INQUIRY

USING EVALUATION TO PROMOTE STUDENT SUCCESS

BEVERLY A. PARSONS

FOREWORD BY GRANT WIGGINS
AFTERWORD BY MICHAEL FULLAN

CORWIN PRESS, INC.
A Sage Publications Company
Thousand Oaks, California

For information:

Corwin Press, Inc.
A Sage Publications Company
2455 Teller Road
Thousand Oaks, California 91320
E-mail: order@corwinpress.com

Sage Publications Ltd.
6 Bonhill Street
London EC2A 4PU
United Kingdom

Sage Publications India Pvt. Ltd.
M-32 Market
Greater Kailash I
New Delhi 110 048 India

Printed in the United States of America

Library of Congress Cataloging-in-Publication Data

Parsons, Beverly A.
 Evaluative inquiry: Using evaluation to promote student success/
by Beverly A. Parsons.
  p. cm
  Includes index.
  ISBN 0-7619-7813-5 (c) – ISBN 0-7619-7814-3 (p)
  1. Educational evaluation. 2. Learning strategies. 3. School
improvement programs. I. Title
  LB2822.75.P37 2002
  379.1′58—dc21   2001004492

This book is printed on acid-free paper.

01 02 03 04 05 06 07 7 6 5 4 3 2 1

Acquiring Editor:	Rachel Livsey
Editorial Assistant:	Phyllis Cappello
Production Editor:	Olivia Weber
Typesetter/Designer:	Larry K. Bramble
Copy Editor:	Joyce Kuhn
Indexer:	Juniee Oneida
Cover Designer:	Tracy E. Miller

Contents

Foreword

Talk is cheap these days when it comes to accountability. Everyone in education makes noises now about its importance and the need to move forward with an effective plan. But precious little has been done to turn "accountability of schools" into what the phrase really means: a manageable and credible system of ongoing feedback. Beverly Parsons has done the remarkable then: written a book chock-full of helpful and wise advice on how to collect information and use it to improve schooling—without overwhelming us with typical approaches to data collection that are neither feasible nor useful.

More important, perhaps, her book makes clear that evaluative inquiry is not an onerous chore. Rather, we are regularly reminded here that collegial consideration of what works, what doesn't, and why is engaging activity—interesting and enjoyable professional work—if we are willing to overcome our fear and inertia to give it a try. In fact, accountability will only become the norm, not the exception, in schools when faculties are invited to become better collegial researchers into their own practice—invited to understand their own effects better (as opposed to being pressured by simplistic directives) as part of the job.

What is true for students about genuine learning is true for teachers, in other words: understandings are constructed—uncovered, not covered—through the asking and pursuing of important questions, in this case about results versus intentions. We cannot reasonably expect students to develop a deeper understanding of possibilities and obligations unless teachers are helped to have the same ongoing experience.

Parsons makes the case elegantly and practically that "professional development" must be recast as ongoing inquiry into the effects of our teaching, in other words, through the use of such tools as the elegant five-stage process described herein. Her book offers a sorely needed map for getting us to our destination in school reform: a place where we constantly promote and tap our collective pedagogical wisdom. She alerts us to a lost truth: The truly "effective" school is not some idealized static institution but a responsive and purposeful place.

—Grant Wiggins
President, Relearning by Design
Pennington, New Jersey

Preface

It's not news that we are living in a time of exponential change. When the education system was designed 100 years ago, most schools were small and fairly homogeneous. A basic teacher preparation program gave teachers most of the core knowledge they would need in their careers. They came into schools with little expectation of having to change the curriculum or even of needing to engage in much more of their own learning. Today's knowledge explosions, new technologies, and global economy set new expectations for teachers' work and learning.

Educators struggle to provide programs that will be effective in this new dynamic era, for they are buffeted, on the one hand, by forces urging quick adoption of new programs, and on the other hand, by supporters of the status quo. While they want to nurture civil, enjoyable, creative, and meaningful learning environments, the means are not easily apparent. Busyness, bombardment, and blaming can mushroom good intentions into a chaotic environment.

Evaluative inquiry—one type of evaluation and the subject of this book—is a process that teachers and principals can use to shift their philosophies and operations to cope with change and to improve learning for all students.

What Is Evaluative Inquiry and What Are Its Benefits?

Evaluation is all around you. Adjusting your speed on the highway to account for icy conditions is just one example of the countless, informal judgments you make every day. Here I present a more formal, systematic process of gathering, processing, and using evaluation to understand the link between the changes you are making in your school and actual student learning. It is a process that schools can use to systematically investigate programs and initiatives to determine their value (for definitions and descriptions of other evaluation approaches, see Guskey, 2000; Patton, 1997; Stufflebeam, 2001; Worthen, Sanders, & Fitzpatrick, 1997). In this book, I use the term "evaluative inquiry" rather than "evaluation" for two reasons. First of all "evaluation" is often seen as something that someone else does "to" schools. Second, the term "evaluative inquiry" balances attention to the investigation itself with its purpose. The benefits of evaluative inquiry are in both the process and its informative results. I define "evaluative inquiry" as others have defined evaluation—a systematic investigation of merit or worth (Guskey, 2000).

Oriented toward the future, evaluative inquiry is about finding what you value and then moving toward it. Contrasting "what is" with "what is desired" involves making judgments but not the kind of blaming and criticism often associated with evaluation. Instead, evaluative inquiry invites self-reflection and offers the perspective of "critical friends" who can identify discrepancies between what you want and what you have (see Preskill & Torres, 1999, for other perspectives on evaluative inquiry).

It emphasizes analysis and synthesis of information (rather than data collection) and places the inquiry process in the hands of teachers rather than outsiders (though outsiders can serve in a coaching role). Because the innovative analyses of data provide a way to interpret data, they help you take advantage of, rather than react against, the national movement toward outcomes, standards, and continuous improvement.

Who Should Use This Book and How?

Many books have been written about evaluation, but typically they are written for evaluators. In this book, I'm writing for those of you in the schools—teachers, principals, and collaborators. Secondarily, I'm writing for those outside the school—in school renewal networks, universities, district offices, professional development centers, and private organizations—who support the redesign of programs, practices, and policies in schools.

If your school is already engaged in systematic ways of determining the effectiveness of new programs and initiatives, this book may help you refine that process. If your school is undergoing major renewal or you are starting a new school, it is a perfect time to build evaluative inquiry into your way of managing the school.

If your school is not engaged in major change, I recommend starting a study group—a small group that meets regularly over several months to discuss evaluative inquiry and to determine how to bring the practice into the school. Even without forming a study group, you can apply the processes described here in your own classroom. Using the basic orientation provided here, you can investigate how the student learning in your classroom is supported by the learning experiences you provide.

Those of you in national school renewal networks, professional development centers, universities, district offices, or private organizations that support schools may find these evaluative inquiry designs useful when coaching schools engaged in renewal, reconstitution, restructuring, and redesign (e.g., schools that are being newly formed or those being divided into small schools or charter schools).

What This Book Is—and Is Not

Throughout the book I use case studies that are composites drawn from my 20-plus years of education-related evaluation. Although the book is built on current theories about social systems, how systems change, and how people learn, my aim is to provide practical guidelines for using evaluative inquiry to investigate the changes you want to make at your schools.

Along the way, I hope to demystify evaluation, to reduce the sense that it is too difficult, or too time-consuming, or too theoretical. I have discovered that many teachers thrive on conducting evaluations—an opportunity to see the deeper meaning of their work and map patterns of change toward their new vision of schooling. It gives them a way to chart a path, to reduce the sense of overwhelming pressure, to be able to monitor and recognize their progress, to enjoy and learn from the journey as well as the destination. With the tools presented here, you will find that evaluative inquiry presents ways for teachers and principals to inquire systematically into progress toward what they value—their school's unique vision of supporting high-quality learning for all students.

The process of conducting an evaluation inquiry, the focus of this book, does not stand alone. Many closely related issues about the larger field of evaluation, program planning, data use, and system change are important. Rather than discuss these topics here, I provide references to excellent resources that already exist.

Why Now?

We are in a time when teachers are taking greater responsibility for student learning, yet confusion exists around data-based decision making and how to make choices among the many new programs and initiatives available. Processes are missing for managing organizational learning and building an orientation toward the future rather than the past.

1. *Changing teacher roles.* Recent reports such as *Teachers Take Charge of Their Learning: Transforming Professional Development for Student Success* (Rényi, 1996) from The NEA Foundation for the Improvement of Education have brought increased attention to new roles for teachers. This book supports the growing movement toward teachers having "whole school" roles as well as classroom roles.

2. *Confusion about data-based decision making.* Data-based decision making has become a popular concept. Yet, much of today's emphasis on data use focuses on the initial diagnosis of a problem. Too little emphasis is placed on data-based selection of new programs/initiatives and insightful ways to analyze their impact on student learning. This is where teachers need more information.

3. *The proliferation of new programs/initiatives.* The wide array of options can lead to confusion rather than clarity. Each school needs its own process for determining whether an option is a good fit.

4. *Lack of processes to manage organizational learning.* Old processes based on hierarchy and control need to be replaced by processes based on collaboration, dynamic systems, and the latest knowledge of how people learn. By instilling habits of self-evaluation and by making systems thinking a regular process within the school, you can achieve a dynamic, flexible system equipped to bring improved learning to all members of the school community.

5. *Need to orient toward the future.* The evaluative inquiry process presented here is guided by the description of your desired vision for your school. When change was

not so rapid, we could rely on what worked in the past. Now the challenge is to face forward. For schools to be effective amidst these dynamic changes, they must make their best estimate of what they want and move toward it even though the path is uncertain and the vision fluid.

It reminds me of the story of the city dweller who went to the country looking for Joe Jones's house. He stopped at a farmhouse and asked the woman who answered the door if she knew where Joe Jones lived. "Oh yes," she said. "Just go three C's down the road and turn left." "Three C's?" the city man asked. "What do you mean?" "Well," she said, "go as far as you can see, then do it again, then again, and then turn left." Frequently, we get a vision as far as we can see based on what our current knowledge is. Then as we get closer and closer, we see something over the horizon that is even more desirable. Thus, the process of evaluative inquiry has a built-in flexibility, an expectation that you will keep adjusting your vision over time and moving toward it.

What's Next?

The book is divided into three parts. Following an overview of evaluative inquiry, the book describes the focus of three evaluative inquiry designs: one to help you determine the QUALITY of your program (Part 1); one to determine its SUSTAINABILITY (Part 2); and one to determine its CULTIVATION of new principles and practices in the school to achieve whole school or whole system change (Part 3). Each part has chapters organized around the five tasks in the evaluative inquiry process.

Each part uses a school situation to illustrate the process. The three schools are composites developed from working with several hundred teachers in over 100 schools through 40-plus evaluations of many types. The names used are not those of real schools. In Part 1, Quality, the inquiry investigates the quality of a new mathematics program at Summit Elementary School. In Part 2, Sustainability, the inquiry looks at the sustainability of an initiative to bring new interdisciplinary content—knowledge of China—into the Clark Community School District. Part 3, Cultivation, discusses Winding Trail High School's involvement in a whole school renewal process. In this case, members of the evaluative inquiry team consider how to expand new principles and practices to move educators, students, and the community closer to their vision for the school.

A separate and concluding chapter looks at how to continually improve your ongoing evaluative inquiry practices. Michael Fullan offers closing comments on how evaluative inquiry helps develop the capacity of the education system to manage and integrate an ongoing array of innovations and choices into its way of being. He discusses how evaluative inquiry helps build continuous learning into the school and is part of the infrastructure of a learning community. The bibliography at the end of the book provides references that you may find helpful as you determine whether the changes you make in your school matter for student learning.

Acknowledgments

Many people have contributed knowingly or unknowingly to the development of the ideas and tools presented in this book. In addition to the published works referenced throughout, I thank the many teachers and other educators whose experiences have been the basis for the ideas and tools presented here. For the Quality design discussed in Part 1, I drew on my work with schools involved in the Colorado Integrated Mathematics Initiative; schools in Washington State that participated in a study of the Math.ed.ology™ program; and numerous schools in state systemic initiatives and other programs funded by the National Science Foundation. The importance of the design was reinforced through my serving on an advisory panel of the National Staff Development Council as it strove to identify professional development programs that demonstrated results for students.

In the Sustainability design in Part 2, I was heavily influenced by evaluating programs funded by the Freeman Foundation, which supports schools and districts as they enhance student learning about China and Japan. Especially influential were schools and districts involved in the China Studies Partnership and the New England China Network, operated by Primary Source, and the U.S.-China Teachers Exchange Program, operated by the American Council of Learned Societies.

At the Education Commission of the States in partnership with the Coalition of Essential Schools, I worked with many dedicated individuals to achieve schoolhouse to statehouse systemic change in support of high levels of learning for all students. Initial development of the Cultivation design in Part 3 was done during my time there. Afterward, the design was enhanced through continued work with schools and communities in the Coalition of Essential Schools; the W. K. Kellogg Foundation's Families and Neighborhoods Program; the Colorado Partnership for Educational Renewal; and the Danforth Foundation's Policymakers' Program to support collaboration between education and human services systems at local and state levels in support of children and families.

In developing the idea of building teacher-led inquiry teams in schools, I was greatly influenced by my work with the NEA Foundation for the Improvement of Education, whose emphasis on teachers taking on greater responsibility for their own learning and for the changes in their schools can be seen throughout this book.

I extend special thanks to the schools and communities as well as to the directors and sponsors of these initiatives and their evaluations.

I also appreciate very much the willingness of Grant Wiggins and Michael Fullan to prepare the "bookends." Their comments help set this small work in the broad stream of work seeking to change the face of education for the young people of today and tomorrow. Thanks too are given to Rachel Livsey of Corwin Press.

And, most immediately, my deep thanks to my friends, colleagues, and family who have been directly involved in the preparation of this book—Carol Bosserman, Pat Jessup, Carolyn Lupe, Clark Parsons, Rosemary Reinhart, Kim Scott, and Kathy Wyckoff. They have contributed greatly through drafting portions of chapters, gathering information, editing, and graphic design as well as through their ongoing encouragement and support.

I hope this book gives teachers and principals tools to ensure that the changes they make in curriculum, instruction, and professional development produce improved learning for students. Because I consider these tools and designs continually under development, I hope to learn as much from those of you who use them and who share your experiences and refinements as you might learn from what is presented here.

About the Author

Beverly A. Parsons is Executive Director of InSites in Colorado. InSites, a 501(c)3 nonprofit organization, assists education and social service systems through research, evaluation, and planning. She focuses on the evaluation and planning of systemic change.

Her evaluation work has involved initiatives to restructure and reculture preschool through university education systems as well as bring about reform in specific content areas (mathematics, science, humanities, arts, and world languages). She has provided evaluation services to the National Staff Development Council, the NEA Foundation for the Improvement of Education, the W. K. Kellogg Foundation, and numerous other foundations and organizations and has worked on projects in Japan, China, and South Africa, as well as throughout the United States.

During her 10-year affiliation with the Denver-based Education Commission of the States (a national interstate compact assisting governors, legislators, and state education and business leaders to improve education through leadership and policy), she led ECS's comprehensive effort to bring about fundamental changes in the education system at school, district, state, and university levels in partnership with the Coalition of Essential Schools. In her earlier years at ECS she served as Director of the National Assessment of Educational Progress.

Much of her early knowledge and skills in assessment, evaluation, and research were honed at the Northwest Regional Educational Laboratory in Portland, Oregon, where she served as Director of the Assessment and Measurement Program and while with the Shannon County School District, serving the Pine Ridge Reservation in South Dakota.

She has published and led seminars on systems change issues and has spoken extensively about them to practitioners and policymakers. She has been on the board of the National Council on Measurement in Education and co-chair of the Cluster/Multi-Site Evaluation Topical Interest Group of the American Evaluation Association. Her doctorate in educational research and evaluation is from the University of Colorado.

Introduction:
Getting Your Bearings

I n this chapter, I introduce you to three evaluative inquiry designs and a five-task inquiry process common to all the designs. By following the scenarios in the ensuing chapters, you will be able to see how school teams can use the general inquiry process to investigate the extent to which new programs and initiatives support improved learning for students.

Evaluative Inquiry Designs

The designs address three key questions faced by leaders of new initiatives:

1. Quality: Does the initiative promote high-quality learning?
2. Sustainability: Can the initiative sustain and develop movement toward the vision?
3. Cultivation: Once on the right path, can the initiative expand to encompass the full vision?

The development of a new program or initiative in a school is much the same as the creation of a new garden. First, the gardener selects *high-quality* seeds and plants appropriate to the environment. In the hopes of ensuring *sustained growth* over the long term, the gardener fertilizes, waters, and weeds the plantings. As tastes and needs change, the gardener may cut back on flowers and add vegetables or replace water-hungry plants with ones that flourish in a xeriscape. Over the years, the gardener continually works to adjust the balance within the garden—*cultivating* the areas with the most desired plants, cutting back on others—so that the whole garden is producing the most desired vegetation at any point in time. Just as the gardener keeps expanding new and more desirable plants and phasing out others, so too the school nurtures new programs to reshape the essence of teaching and learning.

Quality Design

In the Quality design, the core relationship being studied is the one between student learning outcomes and the learning experiences provided by teachers.

First, identify the short- and long-term student learning outcomes. Then work back to the learning experiences that you want to investigate. The learning experiences should be ones that are well researched and based on knowledge of effective learning experiences. The criterion for saying the learning is high quality is whether students achieve the standard that is established. If the learning experience supports high-quality learning, it too is considered high quality.

Since addressing new learner outcomes for students and/or using new instructional methods requires professional development for teachers, it is useful to show a parallel pattern for teacher learning alongside the student learning. The quality of teachers' learning is key to the quality of student learning (National Commission on Teaching and America's Future, 1996).

Sustainability Design

If we are to sustain progress toward our vision of improved teaching and learning, we must look carefully at the infrastructure—the conditions that shape the context in which teaching and learning occur. For purposes of discussion, I have broken the infrastructure into three categories: (1) Structures and Processes (i.e., the formal features of the education system, such as job descriptions, policy, and curriculum development processes), (2) Resources (i.e., time, money, and human resources), and (3) Culture (i.e., the norms, general practices, and attitudes that people create as they live and work together). These features can be very powerful in determining whether learning experiences can be sustained and/or scaled up to reach all students (Fullan, 1999).

Cultivation Design

Now let's talk about my favorite feature of this basic framework. Can we expand progress? Research suggests it is possible by understanding patterns over time that help us "catch the wave" and move to a transformation of the education system. The transformation occurs in roughly detectable stages as a result of collaboration and careful, strategic attention to details. We'll look closely at these issues when we consider the Winding Trail High School scenario in Part 3.

Program Action and Evaluative Inquiry

Typical Planning Cycle

The typical planning cycle consists of these steps: defining the problem, setting goals, planning action, taking action, evaluating the results, adjusting the plan, and cycling through the process again. Although this planning cycle has benefited many schools, I have found that the momentum is lost after the action step. Evaluation of results is often weak or nonexistent. Rather than studying data, the program planners and implementers talk informally about what happened and what to do next. Such informal conversations can be useful, but they are not as powerful as when they are shored up by systematic data and analyses that look at the impact of actions taken.

After repeatedly seeing weary teachers chastise themselves for not collecting data or for not using the data that are collected, I am convinced that something is wrong with the typical planning cycle.

Mutually Supporting Planning Spirals

Rather than a single process, schools need a planning process that consists of two mutually supporting spirals: (1) program planning and action and (2) evaluative inquiry. Separating the two processes helps create a more realistic workload for those involved and draws on the varied knowledge, skills, and interests of different teachers. It is difficult for one person or team to manage both program implementation and the inquiry process concurrently; it is much easier when two different, mutually supporting groups operate the two processes.

The partnering of the program implementation and inquiry processes in a spiral rather than a repeating cycle emphasizes the continual deepening of the implementation and learning. The two processes are led by teams composed of different people, although there may be some overlap in membership. The program Action Team has the lead role with the Evaluative Inquiry Team in support. Both teams report to the principal or another administrator.

Five Steps of Evaluative Inquiry

The five steps of the inquiry occur concurrently and interactively with the program action spiral:

- ◆ Positioning the inquiry
- ◆ Planning the inquiry
- ◆ Collecting the data
- ◆ Analyzing and synthesizing the data
- ◆ Communicating the inquiry findings

Figure 1.1. Five-Step Evaluative Inquiry Process

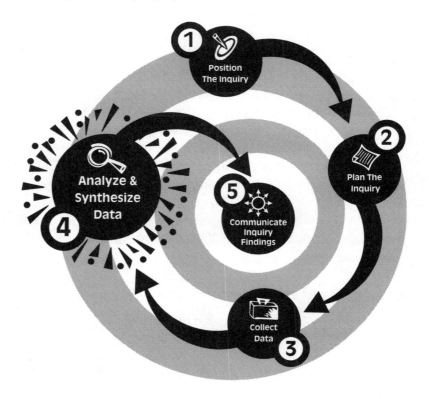

Although I have separated the tasks into five categories for discussion purposes, in practice they are interconnected and often overlap (see the depiction of the five tasks in Figure 1.1).

Positioning the Evaluative Inquiry

Positioning the evaluative inquiry involves three major activities: defining the program or initiative that will be the focus of the inquiry, identifying the temporary Evaluative Inquiry Team, and supporting the program Action Team's development of the Challenge Statement and Action and Inquiry Map (AIM). These activities are carried out in an interactive fashion.

In determining the boundaries of the program to investigate, you will need a defined set of student learning experiences that can be linked to student performance. During the positioning phase, a temporary inquiry team works with the program action leadership to develop a statement of the problem/challenge that the new program/initiative addresses and a useful AIM that includes well-defined student learning outcomes. As you will see in the chapters ahead, the AIM, which depicts the program's vision, is central to the inquiry.

Student learning, rather than teaching, drives both program action and the inquiry. This shift from the traditional focus on teaching to a focus on learning is illustrated by the following story.

One day a man was walking his dog down the street when he ran into his neighbor. He said, "Guess what! I taught my dog how to talk!"

"That's incredible," the neighbor exclaimed. "Have him say a few words."

"Oh," the man replied. "I just taught him. He didn't learn."

Planning the Evaluative Inquiry

The key to the planning task is keeping data collection, analysis, synthesis, and communication well focused on the AIM and the interests of users of the inquiry results. I emphasize the program Action Team as the primary user of the inquiry results because it uses the results to refine the initiative and its vision, to communicate with others who share responsibility for the work, and to refine the evaluative inquiry focus for the next spiral of the program.

Once you've identified the inquiry users, it's time to select one of the three evaluative inquiry designs. The design is based on your key question (as noted earlier) and serves as the basis for determining the analyses. This is a tricky step. In today's chaotic environment, it is easy to get sidetracked from the focus on student learning and the teaching that supports it. Use the AIM and the design to build the analyses, syntheses, and data collection questions; this will ensure a focus on the relationship between learning experiences and learning outcomes. This is not to say that one should put blinders on and ignore unexpected or unplanned paths, but it is to say that following those paths should be an intentional decision. Before following a new direction, carefully think through its impact on the final results and determine what resources will be required for the work.

Then come the practicalities of developing timelines and tasks. These give you a sense of the magnitude of the work and prepare you for the next important decision: budget. You'll want to discover how much time and money you can afford at the beginning so that you can carry your plan to completion. It is better to do thorough analyses, syntheses, and communications on a smaller amount of data than to gather extensive data and shortchange the analyses, syntheses, and communications—the steps of meaning making and use.

Now you can select the Evaluative Inquiry Team. This team should have a deep understanding of the AIM and how to work with data so it can keep the work well focused.

Collecting the Data

The data collection task consists of gathering the data and preparing initial summaries. Gathering the data has three parts: (1) determining who will be the source of information; (2) developing data collection instruments, such as interview guides and questionnaires; and (3) collecting the information (e.g., conducting interviews). Preparing initial summaries of data may involve applying criteria of quality, identifying themes in qualitative data, and/or calculating basic statistics for quantitative data. (I provide only cursory information on these topics because other excellent books cover them.)

Analyzing and Synthesizing the Data

Analyzing and synthesizing information goes beyond the usual data summaries. Tables of average ratings from questionnaires or test scores are meaningless without links to the instruction experienced. The analyses described here also incorporate research about the issue being investigated. The enhanced insights about the links between the outcomes and the learning experiences being investigated will reward your investment of time and resources.

Once the analyses are complete, you will synthesize the findings by contrasting the actual situation with the vision set out by the program Action Team. The differences between the two will enable you to derive ideas about next steps for the Action Team, which might decide to refine the implementation process or perhaps adjust the vision.

There is no shame in adjusting the vision. The vision needs to be flexible. When program leaders articulate a vision, they're setting out a rough idea of where they are headed, not a permanent target. Being comfortable adjusting the vision is as important as being willing to change the implementation process. Remember, we are in a dynamic environment. We cannot expect our vision to stay fixed in such a context.

Communicating the Inquiry Results

In the final stage, you communicate to program leaders the findings that are based on your syntheses. The process brings the users back to the AIM and their initial intentions so they can see what changes to make in their vision and work.

Now let's turn our attention to the first of the three evaluative inquiry designs: Quality.

 **Part 1**

Quality

I n Part 1, I describe how to make an inquiry into a program's quality. To help you envision the concepts at work, I use the setting of a pilot math program at the hypothetical Summit Elementary School (see a description below). Chapter 2 looks at how to *position* the inquiry in relation to the program. Chapter 3 explains how to *plan* the inquiry by clarifying the analyses and syntheses that will be done on the data collected. Chapter 4 takes up the next step, *data collection*. In Chapter 5, I describe the *analyses and syntheses* that transform the data collected into insights about the program being investigated. Chapter 6 discusses *communicating* about the inquiry results with those responsible for the program.

Setting: Summit Elementary School

The Initiative: A Pilot Math Program

The evaluative inquiry accompanies the pilot implementation of a portion of a math program led by Summit's Math Task Force. The Task Force has the charge to redesign the math curriculum and instruction to better meet the National Council of Teachers of Mathematics (NCTM) standards and to improve student mathematical learning.

The math pilot units focus on understanding patterns as well as other math concepts appropriate for the grade level. "Understanding patterns" is a mathematical concept that can be learned at increasingly more sophisticated levels throughout high school and beyond. The Math Task Force developed or selected new units for each of Grades 1 through 5.

The units rely on teaching techniques that are new to Summit:

♦ Manipulatives
♦ Dialogue between teachers and students
♦ Incorporation of writing into the math learning process
♦ Student projects

The instructional units have assessments of student learning built into the materials (embedded assessments). The assessments are a combination of paper-and-pencil measures, largely focused on math computation, and performance assessments, including student projects focused on deep understanding and application of knowledge.

Time Period for the Evaluative Inquiry

The program is being planned in the spring for Phase I implementation in the fall. Each of the following three years will constitute one phase of the implementation and inquiry. I discuss only Phase I.

Demographics

Number of students: 378 in Grades K-5
Ethnic breakdown: 50% African American, 32% Caucasian, 15% Hispanic, 3% other
Number of teachers: 39, including specialists
Average years of teaching experience: 18
Average years at Summit: 12
District enrollment: 15,670
Community: Urban area in midwestern United States

The teachers in this school range from first-year teachers to 30-year veterans. They are cautiously intrigued about new ways of improving student learning. Most teachers want to improve their teaching but want to be sure that any new teaching materials require little extra time for them to develop their lessons. A handful of teachers are very reluctant to make changes in teaching methods. Some will be retiring soon and see little point in changing methods at this stage. Others are not convinced that the new teaching methods are better than the old ones. They want concrete evidence.

Context

Standards and assessments. The state department of education has established student standards in all disciplines. The department administers a yearly assessment of student learning in Grades 1, 3, and 5 in math, literacy, science, and social studies. Based on a review of state assessment results, Summit's school board and district superintendent have identified math and reading as the top district priorities.

Resources. Last year, the school board allocated special funds to teacher professional development and new curriculum materials in math. The district also received a grant to help support improvements in math and science. The district has teams of retired teachers who come to a school to release teachers to engage in professional development or school change efforts. The math support team is available to Summit Elementary.

Inquiry and change practices. Individual teachers bring in new ideas from conferences, readings, and other sources. The school has no systematic means of determining if these new approaches are well implemented and truly improve learning. Because they have seen small improvements with some students, they are afraid to let anything go because they are not certain which of the approaches is making a difference.

Teacher task forces. The district is encouraging schools to set up teacher task forces. Last year, the Summit principal established a teacher task force for each curriculum area. Every teacher at Summit Elementary School is a member of either a task force or an inquiry team. Nearly all were assigned to their first or second choice.

The task forces are designed to both accomplish a task and be a meaningful professional development experience for the teachers. Each task force reviews the state student assessment results in its discipline and determines a plan to improve results in weak areas. The task force also reviews current research about teaching and learning in the discipline.

The task forces increase teachers' involvement in decision making and promote informal sharing—an important form of professional development. A collaborative environment is developing.

Evaluative Inquiry Teams

The district leaders are encouraging evaluative inquiry teams. They want each school to start with one content area. The teams will share their approaches across schools. The district is developing a Web site so teams can share plans, data collection instruments, and methods of analysis and synthesis.

Culture

Generally, good communications exist between administrators and teachers. Teachers work together well. Students feel the school has a pleasant environment. At least some parents are fairly involved in the school. The district practices site-based management. Summit operates under a school improvement plan and has its own planning process.

The Players

Many people and groups, including district administrators, staff, teachers, retired teachers, and resource professionals, are active participants in the Summit program. To focus the discussion on what is occurring rather than on the personalities involved, in the chapters that follow only these few are mentioned by name:

Math Task Force: Of all the task forces in the school, the Math Task Force, composed of six teachers, is the farthest along in developing a new program. The district math coordinator serves as a resource to the task force.

Matthew: Second-grade teacher and chair of the Math Task Force at Summit.

Pritha: Principal. She arrived from a neighboring district about a year ago. She is energetic and well liked by the teachers.

Esther: Evaluative inquiry coach from a private organization.

Positioning the Quality-Focused Evaluative Inquiry

Position The Inquiry

Chapter Overview

In this chapter, I describe how to position an inquiry into the quality of a program so it generates powerful knowledge for the Action Team and other users of the results. Positioning the evaluative inquiry entails three major activities: (1) defining the scope of the investigation, (2) identifying a temporary Inquiry Team, and (3) supporting the Action Team's development of the Challenge Statement and Action and Inquiry Map. The inquiry activities occur concurrently and interactively with those of the Action Team. Effective positioning of the inquiry enables you to link a defined set of learning experiences (e.g., an instructional unit) to student performance.

The chapter includes examples of how the hypothetical Summit Elementary School approached each step in the process.

Task 1: Position the Evaluative Inquiry

- Define the scope of the investigation
- Identify the temporary Inquiry Team
- Support the program's development of:
  a. Challenge Statement
  b. Action and Inquiry Map

Defining the Scope of the Investigation

The first task in setting up an evaluative inquiry is to define the scope of the program or initiative to be investigated. To simplify this discussion, I use the word "program" to describe the set of learning experiences and the defined student learning outcomes to which they lead. The evaluative inquiry will investigate this program's quality. The Inquiry Team will seek to establish a link or correspondence between the learning experiences teachers provide and student learning outcomes while at the same time recognizing that other factors also influence student learning. Although the application of the design in schools may not be powerful enough to establish a firm cause and effect relationship, it goes a long way in helping the team recognize existing patterns and relationships.

The Quality inquiry design specifically focuses on the quality of the teaching and learning. It does not address external factors such as the support of the principal or district policies.

Summit Example

Summit Elementary School plans to use specific math instructional units (6-week units for Grades 1 through 5). Each unit has some emphasis on "understanding patterns," but other math learning outcomes are also included.

The instructional methods in this program are new to Summit. The units call for students to work with manipulatives (e.g., colored blocks the students can arrange in patterns), engage in discourse with one another, write about math, and undertake projects. The new math units will replace or supplement portions of the textbook. The inquiry is designed to determine the extent to which the units are implemented and whether they lead to improved student learning.

Identifying the Temporary Inquiry Team

It is hard to determine who should be on the Inquiry Team until you know what the work will be. Yet the team needs to be in place to figure out the work. One solution to this chicken-and-egg problem is to set up a temporary Inquiry Team.

During the positioning phase, the temporary Inquiry Team works with the program Action Team leadership to ensure a useful Action and Inquiry Map, including well-defined learner outcomes. When selecting a temporary Inquiry Team, look for people who have the expertise to assist the program leaders. This team is likely to consist of two to four people.

Although members of the temporary team may come from inside or outside the school, it is important that one member is a teacher, preferably from within the school. However, in some cases, the member might be a retired teacher known to the program leaders. It is often useful to have at least one member from outside the school—from the district office, a university, or a private organization—who is experienced in evaluative inquiry. Look for people who understand the content of the program and are respected by the program leaders. They should have open minds. Make sure that they do not have an investment in the program that will cause them to bias the evaluative work.

Although some members of the temporary Inquiry Team should be on the team long term, it is not necessary for all of them to continue. Perhaps a person with expertise helpful in planning the inquiry cannot be available for the rest of the work. Fine. Take advantage of the best possible help during the planning phase. It is very difficult to compensate later for a poor design.

Summit Example

Pritha, Summit's principal, asked three people to serve on the temporary Inquiry Team: Esther, the inquiry coach; Glenn, the district math coordinator; and Karen, a fourth-grade teacher who will be implementing the new curriculum units two years from now. Each agreed to serve.

The Inquiry Team will communicate directly with the Math Task Force. The Inquiry Team will have direct access to the principal if it runs into any problems concerning roles and responsibilities. The principal expressed her hope that the participating teachers would see their work as going beyond their classroom role to one of continual learning and growth for themselves and the school.

Supporting the Program Action Team

The Inquiry Team can be helpful to the Action Team as it carries out two tasks: (1) development of a clear statement of the challenge that prompts the program and (2) development of the vision for the learning outcomes, the learning experiences and the link between the two. I call this vision the Action and Inquiry Map. Development of the vision includes statements of learner outcomes.

It is important to remember that these two tasks are the responsibility of the Action Team. The Inquiry Team functions in a supporting role. Let's look at each task.

Challenge Statement

The Challenge Statement presents the problem the Action Team expects to solve or the opportunity it wants to capitalize on. It shows the team members' current understanding of why the problem or opportunity exists. Some people prefer to focus on a problem and consider how the program can solve that problem. Others think of their program as capitalizing on an opportunity to create something new. For example, one group may see low performance in math as a problem and another group may see it as an opportunity to bring in a new way of teaching math. Through the inquiry, the Action Team may develop a new understanding of the nature of the problem or opportunity.

Programs often get started in schools because someone heard a dynamic and interesting speaker promote a program rather than because of a careful analysis of the situation in a particular school. The development of the Challenge Statement is one way to help ensure that the proposed program is in line with the challenge that the school faces. The Challenge Statement also helps anchor the inquiry; it keeps the focus defined in terms of students (see Figure 2.1).

Figure 2.1. Challenge Statement Form

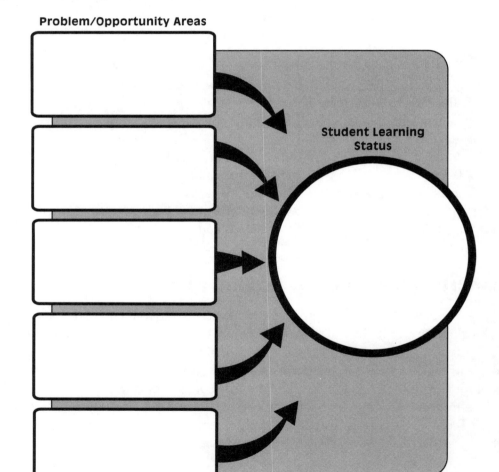

Figure 2.2. Sample Challenge Statement for Summit Mathematics Initiative

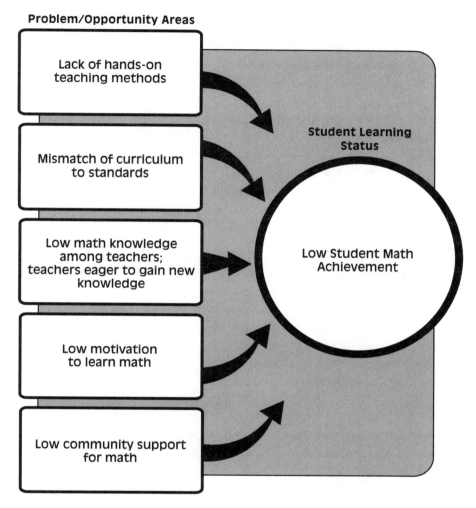

When developing the Challenge Statement it is important to review available student data such as state or district assessments. It is also important to review research on the issue to generate a good range of possible reasons for the challenge (e.g., low student performance in math). It is useful to present the Challenge Statement in both a narrative and a visual form.

Summit's Challenge Statement

Summit Elementary displayed its Challenge Statement as shown in Figure 2.2. In the accompanying narrative statement, the school wrote,

> After careful review of the state math assessment results for our students and discussion among teachers we concluded that we have a

serious problem of low levels of student learning in math. We reviewed research about why students do not perform well in math and compared the findings to our situation. Although we cannot say for certain what factors are causing low achievement among our students, we believe that five factors may be important: We seldom use hands-on teaching methods in math (e.g., students don't have small wooden blocks—"manipulatives" as educators call them—to move around to form patterns). There is a mismatch between our curriculum and our state's learning standards for students. We have had little professional development for teachers to upgrade their knowledge about math (but they are eager to learn more math). We also find that students are not motivated to learn math and the community generally does not encourage students to learn math.

Action and Inquiry Map (AIM)

One of the most helpful roles an Inquiry Team can play is to guide the Action Team through a process of developing a visual picture of the desired relationship between the learning outcomes for students and the learning experiences provided by the program. This picture, or map, expresses the program leaders' vision for the impact of the program on student learning.

Developing the AIM is a key point at which the action and inquiry processes connect. The Action Team needs the AIM to design its program activities, and the Inquiry Team needs the AIM to design its inquiry.

There are three ways of expressing the AIM: a succinct visual display, a narrative statement, and an "if-then" statement. It is often worthwhile to use all three because one method may communicate well to one group and another method work better with other users. The three alternatives also give people with different learning styles options for grasping the vision the program leaders have and how it shapes the inquiry. However, throughout this book, I primarily focus on the visual display.

By the way, you may hear a number of terms such as *theory of action, logic model*, and *conceptual framework* used to describe this type of display. Although there are subtle differences, in each case people are working on a way to depict hypothesized relationships between parts of a program and the outcomes for the beneficiaries—in our case, students. The maps seldom, if ever, fully capture the situation, but they go a long way toward giving people a common way of conceiving of a situation.

Visual Display of the AIM

For the Quality inquiry, I use a very basic graphic for the AIM (see Figure 2.3). (For the inquiries into Sustainability and Cultivation covered in Parts 2 and 3, I incorporate additional components into this map.)

Although you could come up with many ways to display the information, let's use a version that has three basic elements: long-term learning outcomes, short-term learning outcomes, and learning experiences. When developing the AIM, the work moves from the long-term outcomes to the short-term outcomes to the learning

Figure 2.3. Action and Inquiry Map for Quality Inquiry (students only)

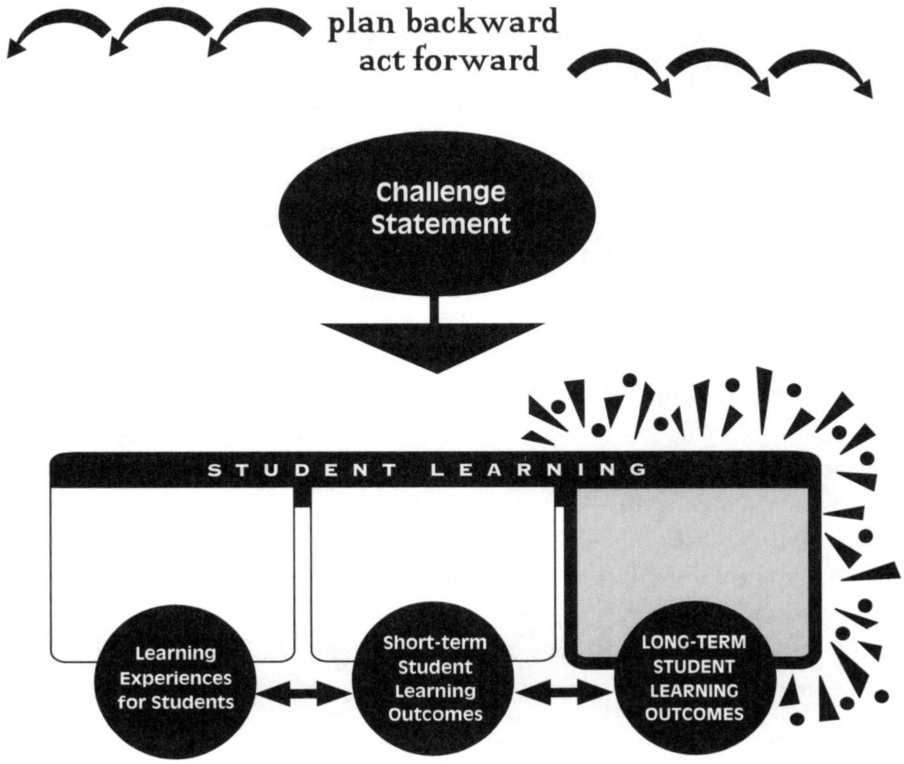

experiences. This is shown by the arrows indicating the "plan backward" process. When carrying out the action, the work flows in the other direction, as shown by the arrows indicating "act forward."

Outcomes

Evaluations often document whether an event occurred, such as whether a unit was taught. That is important, but it is not the outcome. The outcomes are specific changes in attitudes, behaviors, knowledge, skills, status, or levels of functioning for the learners resulting, at least in part, from the program's learning activities.

The outcomes have been divided into long- and short-term learning outcomes. The short-term outcomes are those specifically tied to the learning experience under investigation—in Summit's case, the six-week units. The long-term outcomes are the ongoing improvements in all students' learning of the discipline. (Sometimes, you may want to add a third category of intermediate-term outcomes.) Summit wants to see that the school as a whole has steady increases in students' math performance on yearly assessments for years to come.

The Inquiry Team helps the Action Team begin with the end in mind—desired student learning and indicators (measures) of that learning. Then the Action Team determines what learning experiences will support that learning. Excellent resources, such as Wiggins and McTighe (1998), Stiggins (1994), and Arter and McTighe (2001), are available to help teams define student learning outcomes and measures of achievement of outcomes. State departments of education and private groups often provide assistance on these topics. Thus I do not address this topic other than to say that clearly defining outcomes and determining how to measure them is a skill that is honed through practice. People with evaluation expertise often have considerable practice in this area and can be of assistance as the Action Team undertakes this very important task.

One of the biggest challenges in working with learning outcomes is finding the balance between the specification of the outcome itself and the indicators (measures) that are used to determine whether the outcome has been accomplished. You are all familiar with the ongoing debates about the value of paper-and-pencil assessments as indicators of a learning outcome such as understanding fractions versus performance assessments where students demonstrate the use of fractions. No matter what indicator is used, however, it never fully encompasses the outcome. It is only an indicator of the outcome.

Consequently, when conducting an inquiry, I urge the use of multiple measures. Even then, it is important to not become too tightly wedded to the results on the measures. My motto: Hold tightly to the desired outcomes but lightly to their measures.

Learning Experiences

Learning experiences are the technologies, processes, techniques, tools, events, and other actions that are part of the instructional program. In Summit's case, the learning experience consists of the process of using the math units and engaging in the accompanying activities.

Visual Display of Action and Inquiry Map

➤ Captures fundamental information

➤ Keeps the focus on desired outcomes for students

➤ Provides a common reference point

➤ Facilitates conversation

➤ Shows the whole of the work

➤ Is memorable

➤ Is simple

In the "Learning Experiences" box (see Figure 2.3), list the key features of the program that are expected to particularly influence student learning. These are the features you are focusing on in relation to student learning. (Because the Learning Experiences box in the AIM is not big enough to list all the activities, the management or action plan that supports it details those activities and who is doing what.)

When working on the visual AIM display, clearly focus on the connections between the activities and the outcomes. As people get into detailing the activities, they usually come up with far more ideas than can be implemented. Having a clear sense of the priority outcomes and of the most important programmatic features will help you choose which instructional activities to emphasize.

The visual display serves several purposes. First, it helps keep the focus on the future, the goal—the learning outcomes for students—and the relationship of the program to those outcomes. It is easy to get caught up in the mechanics of implementing a new program and lose touch with the outcomes being sought. Second, a visual display captures fundamental information about how actions are expected to support the desired results. The display becomes a common reference point for everyone involved and facilitates conversation about whether planned actions are likely to lead to the desired results. In later spirals of program action and inquiry, the visual can help you see where and how to bring in new research findings which, in turn, can lead to new types of analyses for the inquiry team to consider.

Ideally, the display should be on a single page and contain enough detail to be easily explained and understood by people who will be associated with the work. Because it is visual, it typically can be easily remembered. If the display has so much detail or complexity that it cannot be remembered, it loses some of its value.

Narrative Statement of the AIM

You may have people in your group whose eyes glaze over when shown anything resembling a chart. If so, use a short narrative that explains in words why the program is expected to be successful. A good narrative conveys the same information as the visual display. It may be more clear or persuasive, especially if it conveys the program planners' understanding of "the challenge," a basic philosophy, or a passionate argument about why certain strategies or actions are believed to be effective.

A Narrative Statement
➤ Conveys understanding of the problem
➤ Explains the basic philosophy of the program
➤ Gives arguments supporting the program's effectiveness

If-Then Statements to Explain the AIM

Another way of describing the vision emphasizes the relationship among the learning experiences and the long- and short-term outcomes. It is a set of "if-then" statements. These statements, which are written out as a set of short bulleted phrases, are unabashedly analytic. "If such and such can be achieved or is allowed to happen . . . then such and such will follow. And if such and such follows, then we should see some decrease in the problem which we are addressing, or increase in the type of outcome we're looking for." Good if-then statements help supply some of the detail missing in a visual display; they attempt to fill in as many of the critical "links in the chain of reasoning" as possible. If-then statements tend to overemphasize a causal relationship. Keep in mind that there are numerous intervening conditions that also affect the impact of the program on the outcomes a student achieves. Yet, if the program provides powerful learning experiences, it

If-Then Descriptions
➤ Emphasize the relationships among the basic elements
➤ Supply detail missing in a visual display
➤ Fill in critical "links in the chain of reasoning"

Figure 2.4. Summit Mathematics Program

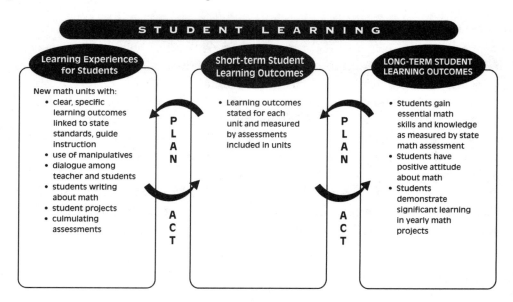

should be strong enough to show a contribution to the outcomes. I find it helpful to think of the learning experiences as having a correspondence to or correlation with the outcomes; that is, the learning experiences and the outcomes tend to go together even though we may not be able to establish a strict cause-and-effect relationship using these inquiry designs with small numbers of classrooms.

Summit's Action and Inquiry Map

Here are the three versions of Summit's AIM. Figure 2.4 shows a visual display of Summit's AIM. The narrative and if-then statements explain it.

Summit prepared both a narrative statement and an if-then statement to accompany its visual AIM display; the school also incorporated its Challenge Statement in what follows.

NARRATIVE OF SUMMIT'S CHALLENGE STATEMENT AND AIM

Our students are not performing well on the state mathematics assessment. Based on research about effective ways to teach math, we suspect that the reasons for low math performance may be a lack of hands-on teaching methods, a mismatch of curriculum to standards, insufficient math knowledge among some teachers, low motivation to learn math, and little encouragement from the community to achieve in math.

To confront this situation, we identified priority learning outcomes for students based on our state's student learning standards. We believe that the state standards represent important learning for our students. We then selected new curriculum units to implement in the fall. These units, which are aligned with math standards, focus on understanding patterns and include hands-on teaching methods. We will pilot-test these units to determine whether they help increase student learning.

We expect that the use of these units will help increase student achievement as evidenced on assessments embedded in the curriculum units and on the state assessment. Through a clear focus on learning outcomes (based on state standards), the use of manipulatives, dialogue between teacher and students and among students, student writing about mathematical understandings, and student projects, we anticipate that students will be able to achieve at the proficient or better levels on assessments included in the curriculum units. In consequence of this improved student learning, we expect to see ongoing progress in students' learning of math as evidenced by performance at the proficient or better level on the state mathematics assessment, positive attitudes about mathematics, and performance assessments that show students' ability to explain major mathematical concepts and apply them in meaningful situations.

IF-THEN STATEMENTS EXPRESSING SUMMIT'S AIM

If we utilize new curriculum units in math that are aligned with the math standards and incorporate hands-on teaching methods, dialogue between teacher and students and among students, student writing about mathematical understandings, and student projects, **then** there will be an increase in student math achievement as measured on assessments embedded in the curriculum units.

If there is improvement in student learning through these methods, **then** there will be ongoing improvement in students' learning of math. Learning will be evidenced by students consistently performing at the proficient or better level on the state mathematics assessment, having a positive attitude about mathematics, and demonstrating new significant learning about math through yearly projects.

Planning the Quality Evaluative Inquiry

Plan The Inquiry

Chapter Overview

Now that the evaluative inquiry has been positioned, it's time to plan how to carry it out. First, I discuss how to identify your inquiry users—and how to stay focused on those whose needs are your highest priority. Then I present two ways of synthesizing the findings from the data; these methods are generic enough to work in nearly all situations. In this context, I talk about the analyses and questions that will guide the data collection to ensure useful information for the syntheses.

The tasks and timeline decisions are next. I include charts to organize these decisions and use the Summit model to demonstrate how a school would fill in these forms. Once these plans are charted out, it's time to confirm the match of the plans to the budget and establish the Inquiry Team.

In practice, many of these decisions are interconnected. So the actual process will not be as linear as it appears here, but my hope is that going through them sequentially will help you determine how to make these decisions in your school situation.

Task 2: Planning the Evaluative Inquiry

- Identifying inquiry users
- Defining syntheses and analyses
- Determining budget/resources
- Developing tasks and timelines
- Establishing Inquiry Team membership

Identifying Inquiry Users

The Inquiry Team is much like a mirror that captures what is happening and reflects it back to the Action Team. The main user of the inquiry findings is the program Action Team (in the case of Summit, the Math Task Force). Two other categories of users are important: (1) the full staff of the school and (2) groups external to the school, particularly district personnel and community members, including parents who are partners in the work. It is easy for the Action Team to get sidetracked into defending its work to other users rather than helping them understand how to be partners in the work with teachers and students.

Defining the Syntheses, Analyses, and Data Collection to Fit the Design

An inquiry into program quality focuses on whether the learning experiences support the desired learning for students. In the Quality design, the core measures and analyses investigate what students learned and the degree of implementation of the learning experiences. We need to know whether implementation and learning occurred before we focus on why.

Often, evaluations of new instruction and curriculum focus on whether the teachers liked the materials and methods or whether the students enjoyed the class. Although such attitudinal measures are important, they do not tell us whether the students actually achieved the intended learning outcomes. We often resort to these measures because good measures of student achievement and the degree of implementation of the new instruction are not available and/or time has not been allocated for their development.

Summit Example

In its Challenge Statement, Summit identified factors other than instruction that could be influencing student achievement. However, those on the Math Task Force wanted to address instruction because this was the factor over which they had the most control. They believed that they could make a significant impact on student learning by changing the methods of instruction and achieving a good match between curriculum and student learning standards. Because the supporting structures (e.g., policies and district priorities) appear to be aligned with the direction the Math Task Force is taking, the Quality design is more appropriate for Summit than the Sustainability design, which focuses on the supporting structures.

Syntheses: Making Sense of the Findings

Just as the development of an instructional program begins with the end in mind—student learning outcomes—so too the development of the evaluative inquiry begins with the end in mind. The Quality design addresses two questions: How do the actual implementation and results of the program compare to what was envisioned? What are the implications for the program's future actions? I have restricted the syntheses presented here to ones answering these questions. They keep the focus squarely on the link between student learning outcomes and the learning experiences provided by the program, followed by implications for the next steps.

Vision-Action Synthesis

In this synthesis, you compare the actual situation to the envisioned situation. The findings about the actual situation are organized in parallel to the AIM, which expresses the vision. I like to place displays of each situation on a wall side by side for the Inquiry Team and Action Team to view (see Summit example in Chapter 5).

Next Steps Synthesis

The Vision-Action Synthesis is the basis for generating the second synthesis—the Next Steps Synthesis. The question you now should answer is "What next steps should users consider to continually improve the quality of the program?"

Notice that I have identified these not as recommendations but as considerations. Although the results of the inquiry are a rich source of information for the Action Team, other conditions and information will inevitably influence its decision as well. The use of the word *considerations* also implies that the Action Team needs to think about and discuss the ideas presented by the Inquiry Team. It may need to interact with the Inquiry Team to get a deeper understanding of the actual situation and how it is different from what was envisioned or how the Vision-Action Synthesis led the Inquiry Team to identify certain considerations.

Other Syntheses

There are two other syntheses that I like to do. The first is the Celebrations Synthesis. It is a synthesis that responds to the question "What aspects of the work thus far are worthy of celebration?" Sometimes, the answer comes directly from the participants in the program. Sometimes, it's derived from reflections by those on the Inquiry Team as they analyze data.

The second is the Lessons Learned Synthesis. It responds to the question "What lessons have you learned through this undertaking?" As with the Celebrations Synthesis, the information may come from program participants or from Inquiry Team members.

I won't discuss these latter two syntheses to any extent in the remainder of the book because I want to keep the focus on the two priority syntheses. However, as you get familiar with the process, I encourage you to consider how to add a few questions here and there in your data collection and analysis to generate information on these issues.

Selecting Methods of Analyses and Needed Data

The Inquiry Team members will analyze the level of implementation of the program and the level of student learning. Because the AIM calls for both long-term and short-term learning outcomes, measures of both are needed. These analyses provide the information for the Vision-Action Synthesis, which in turn informs the Next Steps Synthesis.

Summit Example

Implementation analysis. The implementation analysis determines the level of teachers' implementation of the learning experiences that are expected to improve the student learning outcomes. The Summit team will determine the level of implementation using a combination of classroom observations, a checklist, and a log.

Short-term outcomes analysis. For the short-term outcomes analysis, the team considers student performance on assessments that are closely tied to the program that is being implemented. Although the analysis can also consider teachers' and students' perceptions of changes in skills and knowledge, these are likely to be less reliable than direct measures of the changes. Summit will use the student assessments included in the new curriculum units.

Long-term outcomes analysis. The long-term analysis focuses on results in the content area that are related to the program but are broader in scope. Summit will use the state math assessment results. They will also develop a project-based assessment and a measure of student attitudes.

Link between implementation and outcomes. The culminating analysis looks at the link between the implementation and the outcomes. Methods for doing the analyses are given in Chapter 5.

Developing Tasks and Timelines

Tasks and Timeline Charts

The chart in Table 3.1 shows a general format for depicting the data collection process related to the planned analysis. The chart in Table 3.2 shows a format for

(text continues on p. 30)

Table 3.1 Summary Data Analysis and Collection Plan for Program Quality Inquiry

Analysis		Data Collection				
	Question	Information Sources	Instruments	Time Frame	Who	Time

Table 3.2 Summary Task and Timeline Chart for Sharing Program Quality Inquiry Results

Fill in the names of user groups and your methods and timing of communicating with them during the planning phase. Use the "Major Messages" column after you finish your syntheses to highlight the key messages.

Sharing of Evaluative Inquiry Results

Users	Methods	Time Frame	Major Messages
Action Team			
Internal Partners			
External Partners			

planning the communication of results. Table 3.3 shows a simple format for summarizing the overall timeline for the inquiry.

Summit's Charts

Here is how a member of the Summit temporary Inquiry Team described the Tasks and Timeline charts to the Math Task Force.

DATA COLLECTION CHART

The chart [see Table 3.4] summarizes the data collection for the pilot implementation of our new math units. We will develop a similar table next year when we begin our second phase. We hope to use many of the same methods next year. We are piloting the inquiry process alongside the pilot of the curriculum units this year. Our school is establishing inquiry as a part of the implementation of any new curriculum.

Here are the categories in the chart:

Heading. Since we plan to conduct other inquiries and use this same type of chart, we want to be sure it is well labeled. It gives the name of the program, the type of evaluative inquiry model we are using, and the phase of the inquiry. We are learning how important it is to stay well organized.

Analysis. In column 1, Analysis, we specify the type of analysis for which we are collecting data. The analyses are named for easy reference to the part of the AIM addressed.

The next six columns refer to our data collection activities. We identified questions to guide our data collection, the sources of information, the types of data collection instruments, the time frame for the use of the instruments, who will collect the data, and the estimated amount of time for data collection.

Data collection questions. We identified the general questions we want our information sources to answer. From these questions, we will develop specific ones to include on the data collection instruments (e.g., classroom observation guide).

Information sources. Next, we identified the people from whom information will be gathered and other sources of information. In Phase I, the primary sources are the teachers and students in the pilot study.

Implementation measurement instruments. We decided on three methods—logs, classroom observations with follow-up interviews, and a checklist—for collecting data on implementation of the units (the learning experiences) in the classrooms. The methods in combination give us a variety of perspectives.

Table 3.3 Summary Timeline for Program Quality Inquiry Activities

Activities	Timeline (Months)											
	J	F	M	A	M	J	J	A	S	O	N	D

Table 3.4 Summit Elementary Data Analysis and Collection Plan for Program Quality Inquiry: Phase I (Pilot Implementation), Fall 2000

Analysis	Questions	Data Collection				
		Information Sources	Instruments	Time Frame	Who	Time
Level of implementation of learning experiences	To what extent did teachers implement the units, and why?	All teachers in pilot study	Log	Ongoing throughout implementation	Teachers	10 minutes/day
		All teachers in pilot study	Checklist	Ongoing throughout implementation	Teachers	15 minutes
		All teachers in pilot study	Classroom observation/interview guide	Beginning of implementation and twice during implementation	Inquiry Team members	1 hour observation plus 1 hour summary
Short-term outcomes analysis	(Questions are on assessments embedded in curriculum)	Students in pilot study	Assessments embedded in curriculum	Throughout unit plus culminating project	Classroom teacher	Part of the instructional process
Long-term outcomes analysis	What level of student learning is evidenced in state assessment?	4th-grade students in pilot study	State assessment	Yearly	Classroom teacher	1 hour

◆ **Logs.** We talked a lot about how to make all of the instruments short and easy to use. We decided that each teacher would keep a simple log about the parts of the instructional units used.

◆ **Classroom Observations/Interviews.** Our major data collection approach—classroom observation—generated considerable discussion. Two years ago we probably wouldn't have even suggested the idea, let alone included it in our draft plan. Now we feel that we have all become much more collegial and would like to try this approach. An Inquiry Team member will observe each pilot teacher and then have a brief discussion—interview—with the teacher.

◆ **Checklist.** Teachers will indicate on a checklist whether the necessary materials were available to them for teaching the units.

Outcomes measurement instruments. For the short-term learning outcomes we will use student scores on the assessments embedded in the curriculum. For the long-term outcomes, we will use forthcoming data from the state assessments of all fourth- and eighth-grade students. Recall that when we built our vision we said that our ultimate goal is to have all students at either proficient or above-proficient levels on the state assessments. We do not expect to have much effect on the achievement level of students this year, but we want to get organized for doing this type of analysis. We are also working on the development of a performance assessment and attitude measure to use next year. We don't want to use the state assessment as our only measure of long-term outcomes. It does not cover all the rich learning we want for our students.

Data collection time frame. We propose collecting data via observations at the beginning, middle, and end of the implementation, with the logs and checklists being ongoing processes. We want to keep in close touch with the teachers so that we can learn as much as possible about what is working. Our schedule takes into account when teachers can realistically provide the information and Inquiry Team members can conduct their observations.

Data collection and time. In these columns, we identify who will collect the data and the approximate amount of time it will take.

COMMUNICATIONS PLANNING CHART
This chart [Table 3.5] shows the timeline and means by which inquiry results will be shared with the users. We identified the main users and how and when we will most likely communicate with them. A space is provided to note the content of the message to be shared. This information will be filled in after the syntheses are complete and key messages identified.

Table 3.5 Summit Elementary Tasks and Timeline Chart for Sharing Program Quality Inquiry Results: Phase I (Pilot Implementation), Fall 2000

Sharing of Evaluative Inquiry Results

Users	Methods	Time Frame	Major Messages
Math Task Force	Inquiry Team meets with Math Task Force	March 15	(This column to be completed later, drawing from the syntheses)
Summit faculty and other subject area teachers	Faculty meeting; e-mail messages with opportunity for feedback	April 15	
External partners: district curriculum leaders; parents	Meeting of a few Math Task Force members and Inquiry Team members with district curriculum leaders	April 30	

The reporting of the results to the Math Task Force will occur in early March. Our understanding is that you plan to make decisions by the end of March about the full implementation planned for the following year. Meetings will be held in April with the full faculty to discuss the implementation plans for the next year. These will be followed by meetings with external partners. We would work with you on communicating to the people outside the Task Force.

SUMMARY TIMELINE AND TASK CHART
This chart [Table 3.6] summarizes the overall timeline for the inquiry work. We want to be sure it fits with your action plan for implementing the units. To ensure that your action plans and our inquiry plans are well coordinated, we request that one of the two paid days you provide pilot-teachers this summer includes time for them to meet with the Inquiry Team to go over the inquiry process.

Determining the Budget and Available Resources

Working Within a Budget

Throughout the time you have been working on the above tasks, you most likely have been keeping a rough idea of your available budget and other resources in mind. It is now time to review carefully the draft plans to determine what resources are needed to carry out the plan. Here are costs to consider:

- **Teacher time from the professional development allocation.** Ideally, teachers are engaging in the inquiry work as part of their professional development. If, for example, teachers are allocated 10 days of professional development per year, they may use one third to one half of that time for evaluative inquiry. Some teachers may devote more time to it than others. Determine how much time is needed and how much time needs to be available from the Inquiry Team members to help determine the number of people for their team.
- **Substitute teacher time.** If substitute teachers are needed for the Inquiry Team members, include the cost in the budget.
- **Professional development for Inquiry Team members.** Those on the Inquiry Team may need training in how to carry out their tasks. Include the costs for the team to attend a training session or to bring in a consultant to provide the training.
- **Consultants.** If the team is using an outside coach, the costs of that person's time may need to be included.
- **Travel.** If several schools are working together and are located at a distance, mileage costs might be incurred. A consultant may also have travel costs.
- **Communications.** This includes postage, telephone calls, and so forth.

Table 3.6 Summary Timeline for Program Quality Inquiry Activities: Phase I (Pilot Implementation), Fall 2000

Activities	Timeline (Months)											
	M	J	J	A	S	O	N	D	J	F	M	A
Identify pilot-test teachers	X											
Pilot-test teachers prepare		X	X	X								
Evaluative Inquiry Team develops data collection instruments		X	X	X								
Begin pilot implementation					X	X						
Initial data collection					X	X						
Second data collection						X						
Pilot implementation complete							X					
End of unit data collection (late November)							X					
Evaluative Inquiry Team completes Actual-Vision Synthesis								X				
Evaluative Inquiry Team conducts student focus groups								X				
Evaluative Inquiry Team, pilot-test teachers, and Math Task Force										X		
Inquiry Team completes Future Action Synthesis										X		
Final report of Inquiry Team to Math Task Force											X	
Math Task Force adjusts full implementation plan											X	
Full faculty discusses implementation plans for next year												X
Math Task Force and Inquiry Team share results with external partners												X

- ◆ **Printing and duplication.** Costs here include printing of data collection instruments, reports, and charts, and enlargement of visuals to display on the wall for analysis and synthesis meetings.
- ◆ **Data processing.** It may be necessary to hire someone to perform computerized analyses of some data.
- ◆ **Supplies, equipment, and printed materials.** Costs for paper, resource books, videotaping equipment, or special software may be incurred.

Summit Example

Matthew, the head of the Math Task Force, is an active member of the local teachers' association. The association is working out new roles for teachers to enhance professional development and ensure that teachers play a greater role in shaping the direction of the school. He worked out the logistics for the Math Task Force and Inquiry Team to ensure that (a) the work was valuable for both teachers and students and (b) teachers were compensated for their work. Under these financial arrangements, members of the Inquiry Team and of the Math Task Force and teachers piloting the units use their professional development time or are given a stipend for work that goes beyond regular responsibilities. A school grant pays the stipends this year. The grant also covers the cost of the inquiry and costs of travel, printing, and supplies. Pritha, the principal, is working with the district to include the work of task forces and inquiry teams as an ongoing part of the school's regular budget.

Determining the Availability of Other Resources

Considering other available resources can often reduce direct costs. For example, rather than hiring an outside coach, the district evaluator may be able to play this role as part of his or her regular job. Retired teachers, organized and hired by the district to support professional development, may be available without the school incurring a cost. Community or parent volunteers may help.

When considering whether and how to use other available resource people, consider how the knowledge they gain can strengthen understanding of, and commitment to, the new program or the inquiry process. With first-hand experience, they are likely to develop a deeper understanding of the changes being made.

Establishing the Evaluative Inquiry Team

Now that the temporary Inquiry Team has developed the plan, it is time to select people to be on the Inquiry Team to actually carry out the work.

Responsibilities

It is important first to determine their responsibilities, a typical set of which is the following:

- Review the Challenge Statement and AIM for clarity and logic
- Confirm data synthesis, analysis, and collection plans
- Develop data collection instruments
- Organize/undertake data collection
- Conduct analyses and syntheses
- Prepare written and oral summaries of analyses and syntheses
- Share inquiry findings with users
- Work with the Action Team to incorporate changes into the Challenge Statement and the AIM for next year
- Plan the general approach to the evaluative inquiry for next year
- Determine how to maintain continuity of the Inquiry Team from one year to the next
- Stay within the budget

Membership

Once the responsibilities are clear, it is time to appoint the Inquiry Team members. Ideally, at least some of the members of the temporary team will continue. I recommend that at least half of the members be teachers from within, or recently retired from, the school. The other members could be student teacher interns, paraprofessionals, university faculty, district personnel, or private evaluators.

Summit Example

The temporary Inquiry Team estimated that it would take from three to five days of each team member's time. To release teachers for this work, the district's math Professional Development Support Team will come to the school.

Summit decided to have an evaluative Inquiry Team composed of three teachers, two student teacher interns, and an outside coach. The student interns are being trained in action research, giving them the skills they need for the Inquiry Team's work. It will also give the interns a chance to observe classes with a very clear purpose. Working with university faculty supervisors, the interns will take on the data analysis required to link the level of implementation to the levels of student achievement.

It is important that the pilot teachers feel they are part of the inquiry. So one Math Task Force member and a pilot teacher will serve as liaisons to the Inquiry Team. Esther will serve as the Inquiry Team coach and meeting facilitator. The principal will be on call for the team.

The team will meet in early summer to develop the data collection instruments and make final plans for the pilot. Concurrently, the Math Task Force will ensure that everyone is ready for implementation.

Collection of Implementation and Outcome Data

Chapter Overview

To conduct the quantitative analyses for a program quality evaluation inquiry, you need measures of the level of implementation of the program and measures of the level of student learning that occurs. Typically, you need multiple measures of both implementation and learning. These identify each teacher's level of implementation and each student's level of learning. Then you need ways to analyze the collected information. In this chapter, I describe rubrics: sets of criteria used to identify the levels of implementation and learning.

I focus first on collecting and summarizing data about implementation of learning experiences (e.g., curriculum units) and then on student learning measures. By the time you finish this chapter, you will have composite information about each teacher and student. This information is what you need to conduct analyses for the group of teachers and students involved in the inquiry. The group analyses discussed in Chapter 5 help you see the link between implementation and learning.

For purposes of discussion in this chapter, I use the term "data collection" to include the application of criteria to derive individual "scores" for each teacher on his or her level of implementation of the new program and individual scores for students of their level of achievement of the learning outcomes. In Chapter 5, I focus on the analysis of the group data to determine the link of implementation to outcomes.

Task 3: Collect Data

- Gather data
- Prepare data summaries

Measures of Implementation

I first identify five data collection methods commonly used to gather information about the level of implementation of a program. Then I show how Summit Elementary used four of these instruments to gather information about the level of implementation of its new math units. (Because many other books describe these instruments, I will not provide explanations of how to develop and use them. See page 143 for references.)

Types of Instruments

Here are five data collection tools to consider for determining the extent of the implementation of a new curriculum or teaching practice. No matter what types are used, it is important to record data in a timely fashion and to keep it well organized.

Logs. A log is an ongoing record of events. Typical information includes records of the preparation time, classroom time, lessons covered, and comments.

Checklists. A checklist allows you to take an inventory of the presence or absence of conditions. Simply list the desirable characteristics and have respondents check off those that are present.

Classroom observations. Classroom observations can be done using qualitative or quantitative methods. An observation guide may be highly structured (e.g., requiring a tally of the number of times an event occurred), partially structured (e.g., having categories to attend to), or very unstructured (e.g., placing few restrictions on the observers). The degree of structure is very dependent on the purpose of the observation. When observing the implementation of a planned unit of study, I find it useful to use a partially structured guide focused on the features identified in the AIM as the ones expected to impact student learning. For example, Summit identified dialogue, writing about math, use of manipulatives, and student projects as key features whose use they expect will improve student learning. The classroom observers focus on the presence and quality of these instructional practices.

Interviews. Interviews are an important complement to classroom observations. Interviews following observations help the observers interpret what they have seen.

Questionnaires. When a number of teachers are involved in the implementation of a new program, it may be more efficient to gather certain information from a questionnaire than an interview. Questionnaires are useful for gathering factual information, attitudinal or other ratings, and summary points about events.

Focus groups. Focus groups involve bringing a few people together to discuss the topic under consideration. An advantage of the focus group is that people are able to build on one another's ideas and generate more ideas than they might through individual questionnaires or interviews. The downside of the focus group is just the opposite; that is, individual perspectives may not be expressed as well in the group. Focus groups and questionnaires can be used in combination to benefit from the strengths of each method. For example, after a focus group discussion, the participants can be given a questionnaire to identify the issues and perspectives most important to them. By responding to the questionnaire after the focus group, participants can draw on ideas presented in the group and identify more clearly the issues of importance to them. Another approach is to have participants complete a questionnaire before the focus group meets. The major issues expressed via the questionnaire can be used to shape the focus group agenda.

Summit Example

The Math Task Force left school in the spring confident that the Inquiry Team had a well-designed inquiry plan. Over the summer, members of the Inquiry Team, with help from a university faculty member, put the finishing touches on their data collection instruments (logs, checklist, and classroom observation and interview guide) and prepared a packet for each teacher participating in the pilot test. Concurrently, the Math Task Force made sure that all supporting materials and resources were in place for the teachers to conduct the pilot test.

In the fall, everything was ready for the pilot teachers to start their implementation and for the inquiry to proceed. Faculty and staff noticed a higher level of anticipation adding to the usual excitement that comes at the beginning of a new school year. The Inquiry Team and pilot teachers felt a heightened sense of collegiality.

Ten teachers participated in the pilot test—two at each grade level for Grades 1 through 5. Each Inquiry Team member except the coach worked with two pilot teachers on data collection.

Logs. The Summit teachers kept a log of the implementation of the math curriculum units in which they recorded the lessons used, the amount of time spent in both preparation and use, comments on how well the units had worked for them, and student responses. Each Inquiry Team member met with his or her assigned two teachers at the conclusion of the pilot to review the logs and to collect the logs for analysis.

In addition to using the information to determine the level of implementation, Inquiry Team members prepared a list of factors that had facilitated or impeded implementation of the math units.

Checklists. No curriculum unit can be implemented properly if the units and related materials are not available. To determine the availability of necessary items, teachers filled out a checklist that indicated if they had the materials that were expected to be available (e.g., manipulatives for students, a teacher's manual).

Classroom observations and interviews. Inquiry Team members observed the two pilot teachers three times during the implementation period. The first observation occurred at the beginning of implementation, the second around the midpoint, and the third toward the end of the implementation period. Also, for the first observation of each class, the Inquiry Team member was joined by either the district math specialist, a university math education professor who works with the student teachers, or the inquiry coach. The second time, two Inquiry Team members did the observations in each class. The third time one or two Inquiry Team members did the observation. Some teachers voluntarily sat in on some observations of their partner teachers—the colleague with whom they were matched for the pilot.

The intent of these observations was to determine the extent to which the recommended curriculum activities and instructional methods were being implemented. The guide was partially structured to direct the observers' attention to the key features of the math units that the Task Force had used as the basis for selection—use of manipulatives, writing about math, dialogue, and student projects.

Before going into classrooms the first time, the Inquiry Team met to "calibrate" the observation approach and agree on what instruction at each level of the implementation rubric would look like in the classroom. (The rubric is discussed below.) Most of the teachers in the school (and all of those in the pilot test) had previous education and experience in using rubrics to assess writing. The Summit team applied a similar line of thinking to their observation calibration.

After each observation, Inquiry Team members briefly interviewed the pilot teacher to clarify any questions it had about what they had observed and to obtain the teacher's view of his or her level of implementation. Part of the intent of the meeting was to further develop the sense of collegiality among the pilot teachers and Inquiry Team members. After the final observation, the observer and observed teacher discussed whether the collective set of observations was representative of the teacher's use of the new instructional methods in his or her teaching.

Summary of Implementation Data

The Implementation data are summarized using a rubric to determine the level of implementation demonstrated by each teacher. The rubric is adaptable for a variety of implementations. Two people independently review the data from the multiple sources. The analyzers then average the ratings or determine the ratings through discussion and consensus.

Rubric for Level of Implementation

This rubric focuses on the level of use of various elements of the curriculum units. It is adapted from the continuum of levels of use described by Hall and Hord (1984). As teachers become more familiar and skillful with specific strategies, their level of implementation increases.

The rubric can be used to rate overall implementation of a particular lesson or curriculum unit. It can also be used to rate individual instructional strategies such as the use of manipulatives in the Summit situation.

The boundaries between levels of implementation are not rigid, and people often are not totally at one level or the other. When using this rubric to rate teachers, indicate the level of their predominant use.

Rubric for Level of Implementation

Level 1. Nonuser. The teacher appears to know little about the strategy or curriculum and is not using it in the classroom.

Level 2. Beginning user. The teacher has acquired knowledge of the strategy or curriculum and is attempting to implement it. Use of the strategy or curriculum unit seems forced and superficial. The teacher is exploring the demands that implementation places on the teacher and students.

Level 3. Moderate user. The teacher implements the strategy or curriculum as specified. The teacher adapts the strategy or curriculum unit primarily to meet his or her own needs rather than that of students. The teacher is attempting to master use of the strategy in a specific lesson or to master the curriculum unit with little reflection on practice.

Level 4. Regular user. The teacher implements the strategy as specified in the curriculum and at other times when it benefits students. The teacher is not tied as closely to the curriculum in deciding when to use a particular strategy. Additionally, the teacher varies and modifies use of the strategy or curriculum based on student needs. The teacher appears knowledgeable about the strategy or curriculum unit.

Level 5. Experienced user. The teacher implements the strategy as specified in the curriculum and at other points with the focus of implementation primarily on the impact on student learning. The teacher is able to see not only the short-term benefits to students but the long-term benefits as well. He or she is able to discuss with other teachers ways to make use of the strategy or curriculum in other areas. Additionally, the teacher evaluates use of the strategy or curriculum and modifies its use for different students or offers alternative approaches that will meet the same goals.

Summit Example

Throughout the implementation period, pilot teachers and Inquiry Team members at Summit recorded data while information was still fresh in their minds. The Inquiry Team summarized the implementation data from the logs, checklists, observations, and interviews by giving an overall rating of implementation as well as a rating on implementation of each of four instructional practices—use of manipulatives, dialogue, writing about math, and student projects. Thus each teacher had five scores that could be used in the analysis of the group data. In preparation for summarizing the level of implementation for each teacher, the Inquiry Team members reviewed the logs and checklists to see which lessons were taught and if all materials were available. A few minor cases existed where some manipulatives were unavailable and where portions of lessons were not taught. Working in pairs, Inquiry Team members derived ratings for each teacher. The observers of a given class used the data they had collected to make a judgment of the level of implementation at the end of each observation. Then they discussed their ratings and reached agreement on a rating.

Measures of Student Outcomes

Measures of student learning can be grouped into two general types: performance assessments and paper-and-pencil assessments. Volumes have been written on both types. I briefly comment on each type before describing how Summit used them.

Performance Assessments

Performance assessments require students to demonstrate their ability to apply a concept, skill, or knowledge. Effective performance assessments are based on the vision of what students should be learning. Frequently, a rubric is used to judge the level of quality of the students' performance. The rubric is used by the teacher, student, parents, and others to understand the desired versus actual level of performance. It becomes a common basis for communicating about student work.

Performance assessments can take many forms. The teacher listening to her second-grade students describe the processes they used to solve a particular problem can assess what the children were able to do, their level of understanding, and the strategies they used to solve the problem. For example, a student may be asked to reproduce a pattern the teacher constructed from pattern blocks and also to explain his or her thinking in making this reconstruction. Extending this work with patterns, teachers may ask students to construct their own arrangement of pattern blocks and then to explain to someone else how to make this arrangement. When students have to articulate their thinking in this way, it gives teachers a means of assessing how much they have learned.

In addition to this type of explanation of their work, students can also demonstrate their learning through classroom presentations, posters, projects, written reports, and demonstrations. For an evaluative inquiry, students may be asked to participate in a focus group where they are invited to describe their work, show samples, and provide information on their major learning.

Paper-and-Pencil Assessments

Paper-and-pencil assessments, or tests, are commonly used to assess student learning. There are two primary categories of tests: norm-referenced tests and criterion-referenced tests. In *norm-referenced tests*, a student's performance is compared to the performance of other students who took the same test. A familiar example is the Iowa Test of Basic Skills (ITBS).

Criterion-referenced tests, in contrast, compare a student's performance to a specific set of standards. Many state assessments are criterion referenced. Teacher-constructed tests and tests embedded in curriculum units are common examples.

Various forms of questions are used in paper-and-pencil tests, such as essay, open-ended short answer, multiple-choice, true-false, and matching. These different types of questions assess different types of learning. For example, a multiple-choice question often assesses a student's recall of facts but may not reveal his or her understanding of concepts as is possible in an open-ended question. The multiple-choice question, however, is much easier and faster to score and can provide a picture of student understanding that can be pursued in more detail later.

Summit Example

Both performance assessments and paper-and-pencil assessments were used to measure short- and long-term outcomes at Summit. To look at the link between implementation and outcomes, Summit used only the short-term outcome measures.

Short-Term Outcomes

Short-term outcomes were measured through "embedded" assessments included as part of the curriculum. The assessments were a combination of project-based performance assessments, practical problems that required students to explain their work, and computational problems. Along with the assessments, the curriculum units included rubrics to allow teachers to determine the students' levels of proficiency on performance assessments. Teachers provided the student scores to the Inquiry Team via a computer database, which a retired teacher had set up for the inquiry work. The instructional unit provided a means to derive a summary score for each student.

Long-Term Outcomes

Summit used the math state assessment as one measure of long-term student learning outcomes. Additionally, two members of the Math Task Force were working with the district math specialist to develop a set of performance assessments for use every two years. They also were developing an attitude measure. The project-based assessments will be organized around four key math concepts, such as patterns and number sense. They will involve student writing and/or oral presentation and a practical community-based math problem. Through these assessments, the general public will be able to see how learning is based in real-life situations.

The Inquiry Team had quite a discussion about looking at the state assessment data during the pilot implementation. The school principal receives a CD-ROM from the state with the assessment results by grade and teacher. The student results are reported by learning outcomes. The team was very concerned that the work had the potential of comparing teacher performance in a way that does not attend to other influences on student learning and diverts attention from the focus on the effectiveness of the curriculum units.

The final decision of the group was that the principal would provide each of the two fourth-grade teachers in the pilot study with the results for her classroom for this year and the past two years. (The assessment has only been in place for three years.) The teacher will look at the differences in student results for the skill areas covered in the curriculum unit as well as difference in the other skill areas. She will consider the differences in the classes for those three years as well as other factors related to math that might have influenced the scores. The teachers then will develop an interpretation of changes in scores and what the connections might be to the use of the new unit. Esther is available to each teacher to help with this process. Because the results on the state assessment were not available until June, this work waited until summer. The Inquiry Team made arrangements for a retired math teacher who taught statistics at the high school to work with them in the summer to look at the trends in the data and to develop a multiyear strategy for analyzing the data. They are using methods similar to those developed by Bernhardt (1998) and Holcomb (1999).

Summary of Level of Student Learning

To establish a link between the level of implementation of the curriculum by the teacher and the students' level of achievement requires one or more achievement scores for each student. Often, scores on several measures are combined to give a composite score. A composite score may be developed by simply averaging scores on several assessments, or a process of weighting scores may be involved. For example, a teacher may give a short five-question quiz twice a week and develop a composite score by averaging the scores on the quizzes. Some assessments may measure factual knowledge through multiple-choice questions or through open-ended questions with clear right-wrong answers (e.g., computing the answer to a math problem). Other assessments may measure specific skills or understanding through a performance. These measures will most likely not have a single right answer but, rather, indicate degrees of skill or understanding. Assessing the level of skill or understanding requires a judgment call on the part of the assessor. In such cases, it is important to have clearly stated criteria of what constitutes high quality skill or understanding. A rubric is a means of stating those criteria.

Rubric for Level of Student Learning

Here is an example of a rubric that is general enough to be used in many situations. It was designed to judge the depth and breadth of students' understanding and the quality of their reasoning. The rubric, courtesy of Wiggins and McTighe (1998, pp. 70, 72; used by permission) is as follows:

◆ Shows a sophisticated understanding of the subject matter involved. The concepts, evidence, arguments, qualifications made, questions posed, or methods used are expertly insightful, going well beyond the grasp of the subject typically found at this level of experience. Grasps the essence of the idea or problem and applies the most powerful tools for solving it. The work shows that the student is able to make subtle distinctions and to relate the particular challenge to more significant, complex, or comprehensive principles.

◆ Shows a mature understanding of the subject matter involved. The ideas, evidence, arguments, and methods used are advanced and revealing. Grasps the essence of the idea or problem and applies powerful tools to address or solve it. The student makes important distinctions and qualifications as needed.

◆ Shows a good understanding of the subject matter involved. The concepts, evidence, arguments, and methods used involve an advanced degree of difficulty and power. Frames the matter appropriately for someone at this level of experience. There may be limits to the understanding or some naivete, or glibness in the response, but there are no misunderstandings in or overly simplistic aspects to their work.

◆ Shows an adequate understanding of the issues involved. Work reveals control of knowledge, concepts, or methods that enable the problem to be solved at the intended level of difficulty. There is less subtlety/discrimination/nuance than found in the more sophisticated work, and there may be evidence of some misunderstanding of key ideas. The work may yield correct answers, but the approach/concepts/methods used are more simplistic than we would expect at this level of experience.

◆ Shows a naive or limited understanding of the ideas and issues involved. Simple rules/formulae/approaches/concepts are used where more sophisticated ones are called for and available from previous learning. Important ideas may be misunderstood or misapplied. The student's work *may* be adequate to address all or most aspects of the problem, but the concepts and methods used are simplistic.

- ◆ Shows no apparent understanding of the underlying ideas and issues involved in the problem. Brings to bear inappropriate or inadequate knowledge of the problem.

- ◆ Insufficient evidence in the response to judge the student's knowledge of subject matter involved in this problem (typically due to a failure to complete the work).

Wiggins and McTighe (1998) provide other excellent examples of rubrics including ones for six facets of understanding (explanation, interpretation, application, perspective, empathy, and self-knowledge).

Summit Example

The assessments embedded in Summit's curriculum units included both computational problems with clear right and wrong answers and measures of mathematical understanding that required a judgment call on the part of the teacher (or other person) who was scoring the assessment. To promote the reliability and validity of the scoring, the curriculum units included well-designed rubrics where they were needed. The units also explained how to develop a composite score for each student.

Each student received two composite scores. One score was derived from the computational problems and was based solely on whether the student achieved the correct answer without regard to how the answer was derived. The second score was based on their level of understanding of math concepts; it was determined by using a rubric to score their culminating project and other small performance assessments and then developing a composite score.

Moving to the Group Analyses

Each pilot teacher at Summit has five implementation scores—an overall implementation rating and one each for the use of dialogue, manipulatives, student projects, and writing about math. Each student has two scores measuring his or her level of learning—one for computational skills and one for understanding math concepts. In Chapter 5, these measures of implementation and outcomes are linked for groups of teachers and students to shed light on the relationships between the instructional methods and student learning.

Analyzing and Synthesizing the Data

Chapter Overview

In this chapter, I look at how to determine (a) the level of implementation of a learning experience, (b) the level of student learning ("outcomes"), and (c) the relationship between student learning and implementation. In using the Summit example to illustrate the process, I look at the relationship between the short-term learning outcomes and the new math units. With this information, I go on to show how Summit conducted its Vision-Action Synthesis and its Next Steps Synthesis.

Task 4: Analyzing and Synthesizing Data

- Conducting implementation analysis
- Conducting student outcomes analysis
- Conducting analysis of the link between implementation and outcomes
- Conducting Vision-Action Synthesis
- Conducting Next Steps Synthesis

Analyses

Implementation Analysis

The analyses of the implementation data are designed to help you understand the picture of implementation among the teachers as a whole. I find it useful to first prepare a simple bar graph to show the distribution of the teachers' ratings.

It also is useful to conduct two simple quantitative analyses of the ratings—the mean and standard deviation. The *mean* tells you where the scores tend to cluster and the *standard deviation* tells you how spread out the ratings are (the variation among them). (Other measures of central tendency such as the mode or median can also be used. Likewise, you might want to determine the range of the scores rather than the standard deviation to understand the variation.) Bracey (1997) is a good source for simple descriptions of statistics.

These statistics and graphs usually raise more questions than they answer. It is often useful to have a color or other code on the graph to show what grade each person teaches. For example, you may find that teachers at one grade level are implementing at a much higher level than teachers at other grade levels, but the statistics don't tell you why. Rather, the quantitative information gives you clues as to who to ask for explanations of the patterns you see.

Outcomes Analysis

Now that you have an overall picture of the extent of implementation of the new instruction, let's look at the patterns in the student outcome data. Typically, you want to calculate the average scores and standard deviations for each class of students involved in the study as well as for the group as a whole. Again, it is useful to construct a bar graph showing the distribution of the scores within each grade level. The graph gives a quick visual picture of where the scores tend to clump and how spread out the scores are. If the assessment has an established criterion of proficiency, you will want to calculate the percentage of students who have reached proficiency.

The analyses raise questions such as whether the students who scored poorly in the past have improved. Also, do students who scored well in the past continue to do well under the new instructional methods? These questions can be answered through interviews or focus groups with selected teachers and students (see the

Summit example below) and by reviewing information gathered during classroom observations.

Analysis to Link Implementation and Outcomes

The implementation-outcomes linkage analysis brings together data from the Implementation analysis with that from the Student Outcomes analysis and seeks to determine potential connections or patterns. You need a code for each student that indicates which teacher's classroom he or she was in for the study. This is best done using a computerized analysis program. I recommend talking to your district testing, research, or evaluation coordinator to select a method and computer program. If your district does not have such a person, check with an appropriate faculty member at a local university or see Bernhardt (1998) or Holcomb (1999). If you are looking for a computer analysis approach, check out these Web sites:

www.cse.ucla.edu

www.edmin.com

http://eff.csuchico.edu

Because so much has already been written about conducting these statistical analyses, I will not discuss the mechanics of doing them but simply discuss three analyses that I find useful when looking at the linkage.

Differences by Level of Implementation

The most basic relationship to look at is whether higher levels of implementation lead to higher student scores. The analysis seeks to answer the question "Is there a relationship between levels of implementation of the curriculum units and levels of student learning?" To determine this relationship, you can use several statistics, such as correlation coefficient, t-test, or analysis of variance. Check with your district research coordinator or a university faculty member for advice.

If there appears to be a pattern of higher average scores for students of teachers who implemented the curriculum to a higher degree, this is one indication that the materials are supporting higher student learning. Again, the statistics raise questions. For example, which features of the implementation are most influential? Some answers to this question may be derived by statistical analyses of the levels of implementation of specific techniques rather than of implementation in general. For example, in the case of Summit, the teachers were rated on their implementation of use of dialogue, writing about math, use of manipulatives, and student projects as well as on their overall implementation of the units. By conducting analyses that link each of these measures of implementation to student outcomes, you develop a better understanding of the relationships. Your statistical advisor will likely caution you about the practical significance of differences that you find. Sometimes, the number of classrooms involved in the work is not sufficient to make definitive statements about the success of the lessons but do give clues as to the value.

The statistics give you a general picture to which you can add detail through the focused conversations. In focus groups or interviews with teachers who implemented the program, show them the results and obtain their views about why certain patterns might exist. I especially like to hold focus groups of students to solicit their opinions about what actions on the part of the teacher were most helpful to them.

Differences Among Students of Different Levels of Achievement

You can also disaggregate the student data within the classes of teachers with high implementation. Divide these students into three groups—low, medium, and high levels of achievement. This can be easily done using the classroom by classroom bar graphs you prepared through the student outcomes analysis. With the help of the teachers participating in the pilot study, review the data to see if teachers can determine patterns in which students are achieving at different levels. They may be able to shed light on why certain students are in each of the achievement groups. They also may be able to tell whether students who traditionally have low or moderate scores are performing at a relatively higher level under the new program.

Differences Based on Different Types of Learning

If you have measures of different types of student learning, you can look at whether the instructional methods appear to be linked in different ways to these types of learning. For example, at Summit, the Inquiry Team had two types of measures of student learning—one on computational skill and one on understanding of math concepts. By analyzing each type separately, they could see differences in the relationship of implementation to the two types of learning.

Other Analyses

You may want to do additional analyses. For example, you may want to break down students by grade level, ethnic group, or past levels of math achievement. Your district research office or your inquiry coach can help you ensure that you have gathered the necessary data to make these breakdowns possible. For example, you will need to collect information on past performance in math if you want to disaggregate and look at the data in this way.

Interpretation of Quantitative Analyses

Once the quantitative analyses are available, focus groups of selected students can assist you in identifying instructional techniques that helped improve their understanding. In doing so, it is useful to know these students' level of performance so that you can interpret their comments accordingly. For example, students who did not perform very well may have found certain techniques to be helpful while higher performing students found other techniques useful.

Summit Example

Inquiry Team members worked individually and collectively over a period of several weeks to conduct the Implementation analysis and the Student Outcomes analysis. The student teachers on the Inquiry Team worked with their university faculty supervisor to conduct the quantitative analyses as part of their action research course.

Implementation Analysis

The analyses revealed that nearly all the teachers implemented the curriculum unit at Level 3 (moderate user) and a few at Level 4 (regular user). The average rating was 3.2. The use of dialogue was lower. The average rating was 2.6, with nearly all teachers in the Level 2 or 3 category and one at Level 4. The average ratings for use of manipulatives and use of writing were 3.9 and 3.0, respectively. The ratings were in the 2 to 5 range.

Outcomes Analysis

Here are a few findings from the analysis of student scores:

♦ About 70% of students in Grade 1 achieved at the proficient level.
♦ About 80% of students in Grades 2 and 3 achieved at the proficient level.
♦ About 60% of students in Grades 4 and 5 achieved at the proficient level.
♦ The major weaknesses in performance were in students' writing or oral communication of understanding of math concepts.
♦ Students who previously had high scores in math continued to do well on the assessments of computation, but often had difficulty engaging in dialogue.

Analysis to Link Implementation and Outcomes

The analysis to link the level of teachers' implementation of the program to the students' level of achievement of outcomes revealed the following:

♦ Higher levels of implementation were associated with higher levels of student achievement.

After completing their quantitative analyses of the data, the Summit Inquiry Team decided to conduct four student focus groups to obtain a better understanding of the patterns that were apparent from the quantitative analyses. The team wanted to find out if students could articulate their understanding and talk about what they had learned from the math units. The focus groups helped the Inquiry Team link its Vision-Action Synthesis to the Next Steps Synthesis.

With the help of the pilot teachers, the Inquiry Team convened four groups of students: (1) students who had scored low in math in the past and now did well on these lessons, (2) students who scored high in math in the past and now did not do very well on the measures of math understanding, (3) students who scored average in math in the past and now did average work, and (4) students who scored average in math in the past and now did well. Students were asked to bring along samples of their work as an aid in discussing what they had learned and what had helped them to learn. During the sessions, students were asked to describe one or two new understandings they had about math as a result of the curriculum unit.

Two members of the Inquiry Team were present at each focus group, one as facilitator and one as recorder. After each focus group, the two team members discussed the key points and the recorder prepared written notes. One team member analyzed the information across the four groups.

Synthesizing the Findings

Vision-Action Synthesis

For this synthesis, I like to use both a large version and a blank version of the AIM on which to record the actions actually taken. Hang them side by side on a wall. Using the analyses discussed above, summarize the findings on the blank map. For example, in the case of Summit, the blank map would indicate the overall level of implementation and implementation of each of the new teaching techniques (e.g., dialogue). The techniques that were most useful (based on both the statistical analyses and the focus groups) might be color coded to visually depict the relationship between implementation and student learning.

Next Steps Synthesis

This synthesis can be done in a variety of ways. The most basic approach is for the Inquiry Team to meet to develop its interpretation of the implications of the Vision-Action Synthesis. It is important that the team take time to generate ideas for next steps to suggest to the Action Team. The Inquiry Team now has a deep understanding of the data and is familiar with the realities of its school. The team is in a strong position to develop ideas that will be particularly appropriate. Encourage participants to think creatively and broadly. Also ask participants to record suggestions they have for the inquiry work during Phase II of implementation.

Summit's Process of Synthesis

The Inquiry Team convened in early February to conduct its Vision-Action Synthesis. A large version of the AIM was hanging on the wall and next to it a blank version of the AIM. The team divided into three groups, with each group summarizing findings from one of the three types of analyses (implementation, outcomes, and link of implementation to outcomes) onto the blank chart.

Then each group orally presented its findings, noting where it saw major discrepancies between the vision and the current action. Based on this synthesis, the groups generated a few ideas about next steps that the Math Task Force might consider taking. However, they wanted time to mull over the situation before further synthesis of their ideas for next steps. They also wanted to involve some of the members of the Task Force and some of the pilot teachers in the Next Steps Synthesis meeting.

The Next Steps Synthesis was held the following week with the additional people involved. The Inquiry Team realized this session would require creative thinking as well as good interaction among the group. It decided to have the group meet from 4:00 to 6:00 p.m. with a light supper. This was one of those times those present were glad that the teachers were receiving a stipend for participation in this work and that occasional meetings like this were within the guidelines for the stipend.

When the teachers convened for the synthesis meeting, the Action and Inquiry Maps showing the original vision and the actual situation were posted on the wall. Participants were invited to take food and sit at the table while one of the Inquiry Team members explained the AIMs and the process. The meeting attendees were invited to wander around to look at the data displays and to hold informal conversations with one another about the information. Two Inquiry Team members positioned themselves next to the displays, ready to answer questions.

At 4:45, the group settled in at the table for a discussion of next steps, in the process generating a wide range of ideas largely focused on professional development for each of the new instructional methods, understanding math concepts, student engagement, and parental involvement. At 5:45, the participants were asked to individually spend 15 minutes writing down what they thought were the three most important next strategies, two major lessons learned from the pilot, two reasons for celebration, and any suggestions for the evaluative inquiry for the next phase of implementation. The group agreed to have two Inquiry Team members synthesize the responses and prepare the official Next Steps Synthesis for use with the Math Task Force. The synthesizers would send their draft by e-mail to the rest of the team for review. If necessary, they would meet again to resolve any problems.

Communicating Results of a Quality Inquiry

Chapter Overview

This is the final task. You've done the hard work of positioning the inquiry, planning it, collecting and analyzing the data, and conducting both the Vision-Action and the Next Steps Syntheses. Now you are ready to communicate this information—and how you arrived at it—to those who are responsible for implementing and supporting the program. These are your key tasks:

1. The Inquiry Team communicates its findings to the program Action Team.

2. The Action Team considers the report and uses the information to decide on next steps, working with the principal and others as appropriate.

3. The Action Team and the Inquiry Team jointly decide who else at the school (the internal partners), such as the staff and students, needs to know about the findings and how best to communicate with them.

4. Both the Action Team and the Inquiry Team work with school leaders to determine what and how to communicate with external partners (e.g., district teachers and administrators, school board members, other subject curriculum teams, parents, and community members).

5. Both the Action Team and the Inquiry Team determine the next phase of the evaluative inquiry process.

In this chapter, I take you through the process that Summit used for these steps.

Task 5: Communicating Inquiry Results

- Interacting with inquiry users
  a. Action Team
  b. Partners internal to the school
  c. Partners external to the school
- Determining next spiral of inquiry

Summit Inquiry Team's Report to the Math Task Force

In March, the full Math Task Force at Summit convened to discuss the findings from the Inquiry Team's work. The charts of the original vision (AIM) and the current action were posted on the wall for reference. The Math Task Force will use the results to make decisions about refining Phase II of the program and sharing information with others involved in the work of improving student learning in math. The Inquiry Team plus several pilot-study teachers involved in the synthesis process attended the meeting. The Inquiry Team first revisited the vision for math teaching and learning described in the AIM. It then presented a quick overview of the inquiry process, pointing out the data collection and analysis methods. Next, the Inquiry Team reported results of both the Vision-Action and the Next Steps Syntheses, including suggestions for the evaluative inquiry in Phase II.

Vision-Action Synthesis

The Inquiry Team gave the team a copy of the Vision-Action contrast charts with a bulleted list of key points, including the finding that the four key instructional features of the math units—dialogue, writing about math, student projects, and the use of manipulatives—all appear to be worth pursuing. Another key finding was that teachers need greater professional development before or while using the units.

They need to learn more about the conceptual underpinnings of the math content as well as the instructional methods.

Next Steps Synthesis

When discussing the Next Steps Synthesis, the Inquiry Team made three suggestions:

1. Postpone the implementation from October until January to allow for professional development in the fall.
2. Give teachers the option of either implementing the unit or observing and assisting a colleague this year.
3. Ask all pilot teachers to implement some of the instructional methods this fall so other teachers can observe and get familiar with the process. Full implementation would then occur in Year 3. The team also suggested getting parents more engaged in the shift in how math is taught.

The Inquiry Team suggested that some of the more proficient pilot-test teachers be involved in leading the professional development activities regarding the use of manipulatives, dialogue, and writing for math understanding. In general, it suggested that the professional development be closely linked to the learning outcomes desired for students and that the professional development rely as much as possible on teachers in the school working together and learning from one another. However, the team believed it was important to bring in a teacher or university faculty member with greater conceptual understanding to help teachers develop depth of math understanding. A high school teacher in the district who previously taught in the fifth grade was recommended. The professional development would be embedded into the daily work of teachers rather than being done outside the school. The Inquiry Team encouraged building the professional development approach based on standards of high-quality professional development promoted by the National Staff Development Council and the NEA Foundation for the Improvement of Education (see www.nsdc.org and www.nfie.org, respectively).

Next Steps for Evaluative Inquiry

The Evaluative Inquiry Team recommended that the evaluative inquiry continue during Years 2 and 3 in much the same way as this first year. However, given the larger number of teachers involved, it proposed a peer classroom observation process since those on the Inquiry Team would not be able to visit all the classes. The process would also serve as professional development for the teachers.

The team suggested beginning an evaluative inquiry of the professional development program. Thus, there would be two parallel inquiries going on—one of teacher learning and the other of the implementation of the math program. Those on the team suggested using an AIM that showed student and teacher learning in parallel, thus ensuring that student learning outcomes drive both (see Figure 6.1).

Figure 6.1. Action and Inquiry Map for Quality Inquiry (students and teachers)

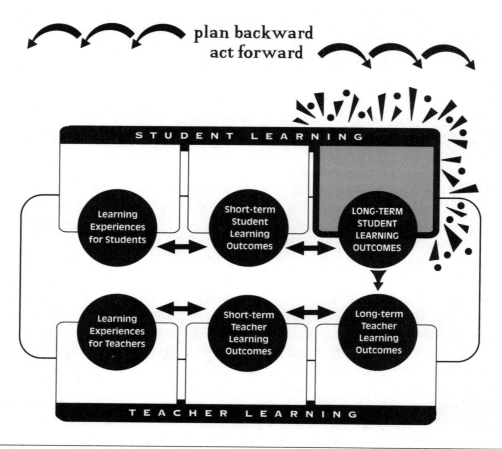

Summit Math Task Force Deliberations

The Math Task Force met again in two weeks to make its final recommendation to the principal for Phase II. At this meeting, it largely confirmed the suggestions of the Inquiry Team. The Math Task Force decided to move ahead on the professional development work as the priority focus but not stop implementation. It also acknowledged the importance of "working backwards" from its vision and making sure that all decisions about professional development linked directly to the learning needs of students. Those on the task force agreed to ask parents whether they would like to be sent materials to help their students with this new way of learning math and whether they would participate in a family math night.

The Math Task Force selected three members to work out a detailed plan of the professional development work that could be presented to the whole faculty at the April meeting. Esther and the Inquiry Team chair agreed to work with the Math Task Force to design an evaluative inquiry of the professional development.

Summit's Internal Communications

The chairs of the Math Task Force and Inquiry Team worked with the principal on communications to the faculty and students. They incorporated ideas suggested during the Next Steps Synthesis about reasons for celebration and lessons learned.

Faculty Communications

They decided the Math Task Force would prepare a memo to the staff describing the inquiry findings and recommended next steps. The contents of that memo follow.

Memo to Summit Faculty from Math Task Force

To: Summit Elementary Faculty
From: Math Task Force
Re: Results of Pilot Test of New Math Units
Date: April 4

This year's pilot test of the new math curriculum units and our evaluative inquiry found that the units resulted in substantial student learning, as shown on the curriculum assessments. Overall, the teachers like these units and support their continued use. Students also liked the units and were more engaged in learning math than in the past. The use of dialogue, writing about math, manipulatives, and student projects all appear to be useful ways to support student learning.

We know some of you, rightfully so, were reluctant to use these units without some indication of their effectiveness. Our investigation shows that these units have resulted in improved student learning in math for most students. We feel that we are on the right track. We urge you to talk with the teachers who piloted the units to get their views directly.

However, a good number of the pilot teachers voiced concern that they were not as familiar as they needed to be with these new instructional strategies and the math concepts that are integral to the units. When they started to engage in dialogue with students about math, teachers realized they did not know the math concepts as well as they thought they did.

Consequently, we are proposing to you that full implementation of this math curriculum be delayed for a year. In the upcoming year, we would offer teachers the option of either implementing the units or observing and assisting another teacher who is implementing the units. Along with this partial implementation we will offer professional development that focuses on both the instructional strategies and the math concepts needed for the effective implementation of these units.

Please discuss this idea with one another. Members of the Inquiry Team and the Math Task Force are available to meet with your grade-level teams to discuss the findings of the pilot study. We will discuss these plans further at next week's staff meeting and hopefully make a decision about how to proceed. Following the decision, a member of the Inquiry Team and/or Math Task Force will meet with each grade-level team to discuss the findings in more detail and work out plans for the next phase of implementation.

Student Communications

The Math Task Force felt that students needed to realize that they were expected to learn math in a new way. It located a video that showed students using manipulatives, engaging in dialogue with one another, doing projects, and writing about math. It ordered the video and will ask teachers next fall to show it to their classes and discuss it before they begin using these new methods.

Summit's External Communications

Once the grade-level meetings were held and plans were formulated for the coming year, the Math Task Force turned its attention to external communications.

Communication With Parents

The Task Force sent out the following message to parents through the school newsletter.

Message to Parents

Dear Parents,
Good news about math!
As many of you are aware, teachers here at Summit piloted some new math units this year. We are pleased to report that students showed gains in their math learning. Both teachers and students enjoy these lessons.
Here is our plan for next year. Teachers who piloted the lessons will use them again in the fall. In the spring, teachers have the option of either implementing this curriculum in their classes or observing and assisting another teacher who is implementing it. In the fall, we will offer professional development for all teachers to help increase their understanding of the math concepts and the approaches to teaching used in these lessons.
Now that we've explained what teachers will do next year, we would like to know if you will be involved in supporting your child's learning of math. We have two ideas. First, we can give you math activities you can use with your child at home. Second, we can set up one or more parent-student math nights at the school next spring. During these sessions teachers will go over

the math concepts your child is learning. This should help you work with your child on the home math activities.

Teachers realize they didn't learn math as well as they would have liked when they were in school; perhaps you are in the same situation. Our teachers are learning new ways to teach math, and they look forward to the opportunity to share these ideas with you.

As you can see, we are suggesting a way for teachers, students, and parents to all get on the same page in terms of the math curriculum. In this way, we expect to see continued increases in our children's math learning.

We have two questions for you. Would you use math activities with your children if we provided them for you? Would you attend parent-student math nights at school, and if so, how often? Please fill out the form below and mail it back to the school or call the school office to let us know your answers to these questions.

Communications to the District Office and Other Schools

Matthew, chair of the Math Task Force, and the principal met with the district math specialist to review their decisions. They also met with task force leaders and principals from other schools who were piloting changes in other subject areas. In this way, schools in the district are learning from one another's experiences.

Epilogue

Some time later, Matthew e-mailed Esther, the inquiry coach, writing, "I think we are well on our way to carrying out most of the evaluative inquiry ourselves for the next couple years. However, we would like to have you review our data collection instruments in the professional development area and help facilitate our data analyses and syntheses. Would you have time for that?"

Esther e-mailed back, "Sure, I would be happy to assist in whatever way you would like. I am very impressed with the way your team has taken on the inquiry task. I agree that you are ready to move ahead largely on your own. I feel most successful in this work when I have worked myself out of a job."

 **Part 2**

Sustainability

An Inquiry Into an Initiative's Sustainability

Part 1 described the most basic and important evaluative inquiry design: the Quality design. It looked at the quality of the learning for both teachers and students. If a program or initiative does not produce high-quality learning for students, there is little point in sustaining or expanding it. Yet, high-quality learning is not sufficient to ensure continuation of an initiative.

In Part 2, I present an inquiry design that focuses on the sustainability of the initiative. The design incorporates an emphasis on student and teacher learning but goes beyond learning to look at the infrastructure—the structures, processes, resources, and climate that surround it. It asks the question: Is this environment supporting and nurturing the program or initiative?

Consider our garden analogy again. Jim and Maria first find the mix of vegetables and flowers they want to grow based on what their family finds attractive. They look for the best seeds for their soil and other conditions. Once the seeds are planted and begin to sprout, they attend to the surrounding conditions on an ongoing basis. They focus on the conditions they can adjust: amount of water, shade, fertilizer, and weeding. When selecting more seeds, they work back and forth between the quality of the seeds and the supportive nature of the surrounding conditions for growth.

So too, once a school has selected effective learning experiences for students and appropriate professional development for teachers, the challenge is to ensure that the surrounding conditions nurture the learning.

I illustrate the Sustainability design in Part 2 with the hypothetical Clark Community School District's initiative to bring China into its curriculum (see the description of the setting below). As in Part 1, the chapters are organized around the five steps in the evaluative inquiry process, although some chapters cover more than one step. Chapter 7 looks at how to position the evaluative inquiry in relation to the initiative. Chapter 8 takes up the next step: how to plan the inquiry. Chapter 9 explains data collection and analysis processes, and Chapter 10 describes the syntheses that provide information to support communicating about the inquiry results with those responsible for the initiative. The different focus for the inquiry leads to different analyses than in the Quality inquiry design, which in turn leads to different data collection activities.

Setting: Clark Community School District

The Initiative: China in the Curriculum

Educators within Clark Community School District are building an emphasis on China into the curriculum across subject areas and grade levels in a way that supports important student and teacher learning about China. The Clark Community initiative is at an earlier stage of development than Summit's math program. Summit was clear on its desired student learning outcomes regarding math. Clark Community School District is not yet clear about the outcomes regarding China or the status of instruction about China.

Time Period for the Evaluative Inquiry

In October, Clark Community began consideration of an evaluative inquiry that would help it develop a strategy to sustain high-quality learning about China. It took until January to appropriately position the evaluative inquiry. The district developed its specific evaluative inquiry plan in January and collected data in February and March. It analyzed and synthesized the data in March and early April with communication of results in April through the end of the school year. Communications continued the next fall along with planning for a new round of inquiry.

Demographics

Number of students in district: 8,530

Ethnic breakdown: 42% Caucasian, 25% Asian American, 12% African American, 18% Hispanic, and 3% other

Number of teachers: 580

Average years of teaching experience: 17

Average years in Clark Community School District: 12

Schools: Six elementary schools, three middle schools, and two high schools

Community: Suburb of large metropolitan area in eastern United States, wide economic span

Context

Standards, Curriculum, and Assessment

The state has student standards in all disciplines. China is addressed in a minimal way in the social studies standards. It is not mentioned in other content areas.

There are publicly reported state assessments in reading, math, writing, and science. A controversial state assessment in social studies is under development.

China is taught at a few grade levels in the Clark Community schools but no one is clear on the extent to which it is taught across all schools.

Planning and Decision Making

Clark Community School District has a districtwide Strategic Planning Committee. Schools also have planning groups. Decisions about curriculum and assessment are a mix of school-based and districtwide decisions.

Professional Development

The teachers' association, a strong advocate of professional development, negotiated with the district for 10 days of professional development annually for each teacher. Additional days are available for special school or districtwide committee work focused on improved student learning.

Resources

The district largely devotes its regular resources to its top priority: improving student performance in reading, writing, and math. The district has a few private foundation grants.

Collaborators

Clark Community School District and eight nearby districts work in partnership with the China Consortium, a local nonprofit organization, to provide professional development for educators related to China. Over a dozen Clark Community educators have participated in the seminars, workshops, and study tours. This work is funded by a private foundation.

Key Administrators

Clark Community School District's superintendent is fairly traditional. However, he recently participated in a China Consortium study tour to China along with several other local superintendents. He returned convinced of the importance of China in today's economic and political situation and is eager to encourage more student and teacher learning about China.

The district's curriculum director is well liked. She is eager to encourage more project-based learning and performance assessments. She has considerable background in planning and development of learning outcomes.

The Players

The following people are involved in the Clark Community scenario:

Christine: Clark Community School District curriculum director; co-chair of the Clark Community China Task Force (CCC Task Force)

Esther: Evaluative inquiry coach from a private organization
Joseph: Social studies teacher at Clark Community South Middle School
Lu Fan: District research director; member of Inquiry Team
Ricardo: Principal; member of Inquiry Team
Milton: Principal of North Middle School; co-chair of CCC Task Force

Positioning the Sustainability Inquiry

Chapter Overview

In this chapter, I explain how to position a Sustainability evaluative inquiry with a balanced emphasis on infrastructure, student learning, and teacher learning. Like the Quality-focused inquiry, positioning the Sustainability inquiry entails three major activities: (1) defining the scope of the investigation and the users of the information; (2) identifying a temporary Inquiry Team; and (3) supporting the Action Team's development of its Challenge Statement and AIM. However, these activities are more complex in a Sustainability-focused inquiry because more features of the situation are addressed.

Defining the Initiative: Clark Community School District Example

Let's explore how Clark Community schools got started on their inquiry and defined the scope of the investigation by "listening" in on an e-mail conversation between Joseph, a teacher at a Clark Community school, and Esther, an inquiry coach. Later, Christine, the district's curriculum director, gets involved.

FROM: Joseph
DATE: October 2
Esther, do you remember me? I was a member of the Summit Elementary School Inquiry Team. I was very impressed with the changes made in the math program, including the professional development process we put in place.

I moved to the other side of the state. The population here is much more diverse. People range from those whose ancestors came over on the Mayflower to recent immigrants from Southeast Asia, Central America, and Puerto Rico, many of whom are just learning English.

I'm teaching social studies at the middle school here (I received my social studies certification last year). I walked into a very interesting situation. The superintendent, curriculum director, and two teachers went to China last year. Other teachers attended three-week summer institutes about China over the past two years. The push is on to incorporate China into the curriculum. China is crucial in this global society. Right now the school curricula are very Eurocentric.

Of course, everyone seems to think social studies is the place for China in the curriculum, but, wow, we have so much to teach. I don't know how to integrate it in a way that will have a lasting impact on the kids. After the work we did in math at Summit, I'm very leery about just adding in a few lessons on China at one or two grade levels and expecting it to matter.

I talked with the principal about the inquiry work we did at Summit. He suggested I talk to the district curriculum director to see if she would build in a systematic inquiry process. Would we use the same general design we used at Summit?

Design Choice

FROM: Esther
DATE: October 3
I suspect you need a different design—a sustainability design—because of differences in the infrastructure supporting a China-related curriculum from that supporting math in the curriculum.

FROM: Joseph
DATE: October 3
What do you mean by "infrastructure"?

FROM: Esther
DATE: October 3
Oops. By infrastructure, I mean the planning processes, allocation of resources, nature of leadership, collaborations with universities, policies of the school or district (e.g., for curriculum content, hiring), resources, and general culture or climate of the school. Basically, the infrastructure includes the often invisible structures, practices, and conditions that shape the classroom experiences of teachers and students.

Infrastructure Differences

Here are examples of the infrastructure differences affecting Summit's math program and Clark Community's China program that led me to suggest a Sustainability design rather than a Quality design for Clark Community.

Emphasis in State Standards

First of all, math is a high priority due to state standards. Also, it is taught to all students up through eighth grade. On the other hand, if China is included in the state standards and/or taught, it is likely one of many topics in the social studies curriculum. It might be taught for two to six weeks in the second, third, or fourth grade and perhaps again once in middle school for about the same amount of time. One time it may be included in the study of ancient cultures and another time within geography. It is only one of many cultures and geographic locations briefly touched on.

Teachers' Knowledge

Another difference is in the teachers' knowledge about China. The math teacher has had a decent amount of education in math while even the social studies teachers, let alone other teachers, may have had no specific education related to China.

Community Valuing and Resources

The typical community's valuing of the two areas is markedly different. The community values the teaching of math while most community members have scarcely thought about the importance of China in the curriculum. The amount of resources devoted to the two subjects is markedly different.

Assessment

And finally, here's a big one—the state assessment. Every state assessment I have seen includes math as an area of assessment. If China is even addressed in the state assessment, it is addressed in a couple of questions within the social studies assessment. Many states are still arguing over the content for the social studies assessment, have put it on the back burner, or do not plan to assess it. What does that tell you about its priority and your ability to track the impact of curriculum changes over many years?

Moving China into the curriculum requires clear standards for student learning, effective learning experiences, and professional development for teachers. Issues of priorities, resource allocation, and community norms are shaped by the infrastructure of the education system. To move new content into the curriculum that is not emphasized by state standards and assessment and does not have widespread community support and financial backing usually entails adjustments in the infrastructure, as well as in what and how students and teachers learn.

But before we discuss the design further, we need to step back and address a few other issues, for example, who is going to use the results of the inquiry?

Users

FROM: Joseph
DATE: October 4
The results will be used by those who want to bring China into the curriculum. We want to figure out how to be sure our efforts are not wasted. I think we are interested in both the quality of the content now being taught and the infrastructure that supports it.

FROM: Esther
DATE: October 4
Is there an official committee working on bringing China into the curriculum?

FROM: Joseph
DATE: October 5
No, I don't think so. It seems to be just an informal group of administrators and teachers who are excited about the idea.

FROM: Esther
DATE: October 5
It's great to have an enthusiastic group of educators. They are essential for making change. But I'm nervous about designing an inquiry without knowing whether the group has the decision-making power to use the results.

FROM: Joseph
DATE: October 6
That makes good sense. I'm going over to the district office tomorrow after my last class to talk with the curriculum director about the inquiry possibilities. I'll talk with her about this.

FROM: Joseph
DATE: October 8
I met with Christine, our district curriculum director. She was intrigued by what I had to say about an evaluative inquiry. I emphasized that when I was at

Summit we planned backward from the student learning outcomes. She said that although the planning backward idea has been around for a number of years, it is just starting to reach the classroom in this district. If we can approach the new emphasis on China from this perspective, maybe the approach can be carried over into other subject areas.

Christine would like to talk with you directly about how to proceed. I gave her your phone number and e-mail address. I expect you'll hear from her soon.

FROM: Christine (to Esther)
DATE: October 9
Joseph Cordova talked to me about an evaluative inquiry we might undertake as we bring China into the curriculum of our schools. As long as I have been in education, I have never been involved in bringing a critical, underappreciated, cross-disciplinary new body of knowledge into the system. I know there are many factors to take into account. I think the inquiry process could be very helpful. Would you be able to help us develop an inquiry design for this effort?

FROM: Esther
DATE: October 11
Yes, I would enjoy working with you. Do you have a task force or other group that is guiding the overall strategy for bringing China into the curriculum?

FROM: Christine
DATE: October 12
I'm embarrassed to say that we don't have such a group. Until we started talking about the evaluative inquiry, I hadn't recognized that we were proceeding on this work in such an ad hoc way. The superintendent and I, along with the teachers who went to China, have had many conversations about it and are talking it up among people we meet. We have made presentations to the school board. They are very supportive, but we have not asked them officially to support the work and we have not made a decision among our Management Team about this. We had better make this a bit more formal before we even think about the inquiry plan.

It is beginning to dawn on me that we don't have processes in the district for bringing in new interdisciplinary content. We have ways to update what we are doing in defined disciplines but to bring in a new content that cuts across disciplines, hmm, we aren't set up for that.

I'm in a study group with curriculum directors from neighboring districts. We are looking at the rapid changes in society and the implications for schools. I realize now that one of the implications is that we need new processes to manage our work. We need processes, such as evaluative inquiry, that make the education system more flexible. I want to combine evaluative inquiry with the process of setting up task forces to guide the introduction of new interdisciplinary content into the curriculum. Let me get back to you after I talk with the superintendent.

FROM: Christine
DATE: October 25
It took me two weeks to get a plan worked out with the superintendent about the China work. Here's what we decided. I'll appoint a temporary task force to work with me to determine whether and how we proceed to bring China into the curriculum. Give me another month or so before we talk about the evaluative inquiry. I have to first get clear on who the decision makers will be so they can determine what inquiry is useful to them.

FROM: Esther
DATE: October 26
That's fine. Take as long as you need. It's important to have a clear sense of what it is you are evaluating and who will be the recipient of the new knowledge gained through the inquiry. Sometimes, an Inquiry Team is set up too early. It becomes the manager, instead of the evaluator, of the work.

Since you are experienced in developing student learning outcomes, I'll send you some materials that you might want to use with the Task Force to define a Challenge Statement and develop an Action and Inquiry Map. Often, the Inquiry Team assists a decision-making group such as your Task Force to develop these but there is no need for that if members of the Task Force such as yourself already have the skills to do that work.

FROM: Christine
DATE: October 27
Thanks for the materials. I like the approach to defining a Challenge Statement and Action and Inquiry Map. We hope we can use them once we figure out how to organize our work.

FROM: Christine
DATE: December 9
Thanks for your patience. Looking at my saved mail, I see that it has been six weeks since we last communicated. The time was well spent.

The superintendent asked the school board for its approval to establish the Clark Community China Task Force. The Task Force has been appointed by the superintendent and given the authority to develop and pilot-test approaches to bring China into the curriculum. I am responsible for setting general parameters for their work. Each school also is setting up a China committee. The superintendent has a discretionary fund that will support this work.

The teachers who have been to China, the principals of our 11 schools, and several teachers who are known as opinion leaders are on the Task Force. We have representation from all disciplines. Milton, principal of North Middle School, and I are co-chairing the Task Force.

I have done a lot of work in developing student learning outcomes and action plans. I was able to work with the Task Force to develop the Challenge Statement and the Action and Inquiry Map based on the materials you sent me.

The Task Force is now ready to set up an evaluative inquiry. Could you come to a Task Force meeting after the winter vacation to discuss the inquiry process?

FROM: Esther
DATE: December 20
Sure. I can give the Task Force an overview of the whole process. Then we can discuss next steps.

Identifying the Temporary Inquiry Team

Points to Consider

The temporary Inquiry Team's role in the Sustainability design is similar to its role in the Quality design. It works with the initiative leaders as needed to refine the Challenge Statement and the AIM and then plans the inquiry.

The Inquiry Team for the Sustainability design is likely to have a different mix of people from the one for the Quality design. Because the Sustainability design includes an emphasis on the infrastructure of the district and schools, it is important to involve one or more administrators familiar with the infrastructure.

Clark Community Example

Lu Fan, the district research director, who has a strong background in evaluation; Joseph, a teacher; and Ricardo, a principal from one of the schools who is a member of his school's China committee, served as the temporary Inquiry Team. This group brought perspectives from multiple levels of the education system.

Developing the Challenge Statement and AIM

Points to Consider

Developing an AIM for a Sustainability inquiry design is similar to developing one for the Quality design. However, the Sustainability design has the added component of the infrastructure's impact on the initiative. You can think of this vision framework as having three major parts: (a) teaching and learning for students, (b) professional development for teachers, and (c) the infrastructure.

Components of the Infrastructure

There are many ways to categorize components of the infrastructure. I like to use the three categories of structures/processes, resources, and culture. They highlight who needs to take action to bring about changes. Structures and processes are shaped largely by the bureaucracy that defines the education system, with administrators and policymakers being the primary decision makers. Although resources are heavily influenced by administrative and policy decisions, I like to identify them as a separate category to emphasize different types of resources and their uses. The third category, culture, is determined largely by informal interactions, attitudes, and norms rather than by policy. Informal and formal leaders as well as other factors shape the culture. The culture of both the school and community are important. I like Schein's (1985) definition of culture: "The deeper level of basic assumptions and beliefs that are shared by members of an organization, that operate unconsciously, and that define in a basic 'take-for-granted' fashion an organization's view of itself and its environment" (p. 6).

Figure 7.1 presents a visual way of thinking about the relationship of the infrastructure to the learning outcomes and learning experiences of both teachers and students. The figure is an extension of Figure 6.1, which depicts the Quality evaluative inquiry. Figure 7.1 shows that both student and teacher learning are driven by desired student outcomes. The infrastructure needs to support achievement of the desired learning by both students and teachers.

This is one more version of planning backward from the desired student learning. This version of planning backward, however, is more complicated than the instructional planning backward because the infrastructure supports far more than the one initiative that is being investigated. It is important to keep this issue in mind as you investigate the infrastructure for a given initiative.

Alternative Action and Inquiry Maps

In Part 1, I recommended using a narrative statement and if-then statement of the Action and Inquiry Map in addition to the graphic display. The Sustainability inquiry uses these too, but yet another alternative may help explain the complexity of this design—an analogy in pictorial form. For example, a visual of a few flowers in a garden showing how they draw on nutrients from the soil and air might be used. The flowers represent the teaching and learning, and the nutrients represent support from the infrastructure.

Clark Community Example

The Clark Community China Task Force (CCC Task Force) didn't need help from the temporary Inquiry Team because Christine was able to guide the development of the Challenge Statement and AIM.

Before developing the Challenge Statement and AIM, the CCC Task Force asked principals to identify where China currently was taught in their school and what skills, knowledge, and attitudes students were to acquire.

The CCC Task Force found that China is covered in geography in the fourth grade, and ancient China is taught in the sixth grade. In high school, China is addressed in an elective course on Asian Studies and covered lightly in tenth-grade world history. That is about it. No school has learning outcomes specifically related to China. The music, art, literature, health, and physical education teachers were

Figure 7.1. Action and Inquiry Map for Sustainability Inquiry (students and teachers)

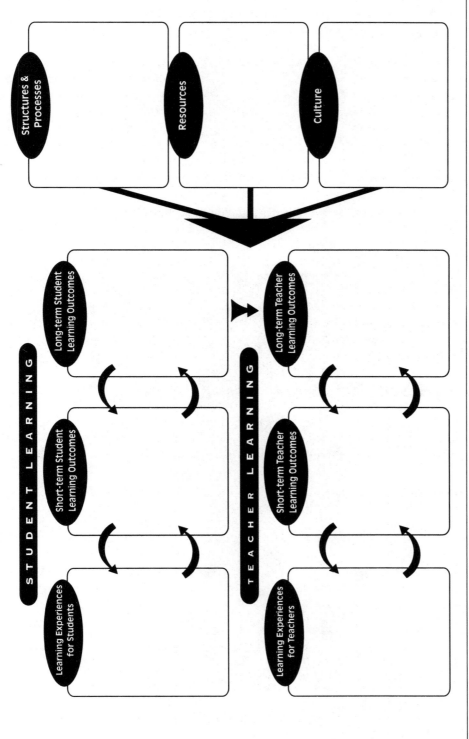

intrigued with the idea of teaching important skills based in Chinese culture and practices. The middle and high school math and science teachers were not keen on the idea.

Challenge Statement

To develop its Challenge Statement, the CCC Task Force invited members of the school-level China committees to an orientation meeting at which an expert on the role of China in today's society spoke. Following his presentation, the group developed the Challenge Statement. Figure 7.2 represents this statement.

Figure 7.2. Clark Community School District Challenge Statement

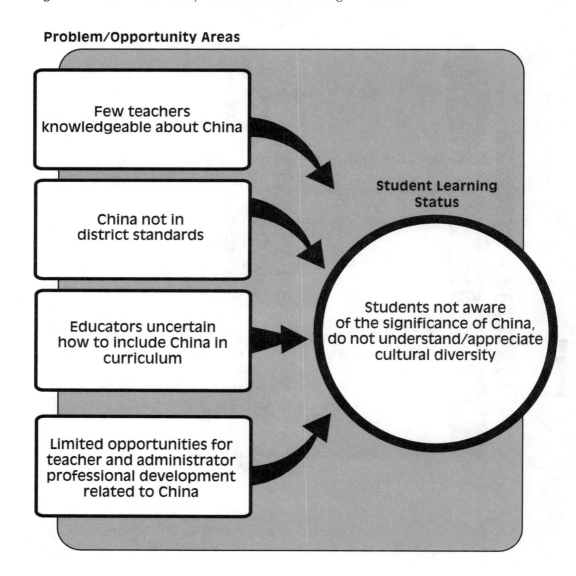

Problem/Opportunity Areas

Few teachers knowledgeable about China

China not in district standards

Educators uncertain how to include China in curriculum

Limited opportunities for teacher and administrator professional development related to China

Student Learning Status

Students not aware of the significance of China, do not understand/appreciate cultural diversity

Action and Inquiry Map

The first step in developing the AIM is to define student learning outcomes.

Long-term learning outcomes. The CCC Task Force agreed on two major outcomes for student learning: (a) All students will understand and appreciate Chinese culture, and (b) all students will understand the influence of Asia on the global economy. They want students to learn about a variety of cultures. Chinese culture is a high priority because of its population size and its expanding role in the world. Those on the CCC Task Force felt that all teachers should gain some understanding about China as it related to their discipline. However, they do not want to lock this plan in place until the inquiry is complete.

Short-term learning outcomes. The CCC Task Force had a lively discussion about what skills and knowledge should be identified within courses as the short-term outcomes that build toward the two long-term outcomes. Generally speaking, the district organizes outcomes into three categories: knowledge that students are familiar with but do not learn in depth; important knowledge (facts, concepts, and principles) and skills (processes, strategies, and methods) to accomplish key performances; and deep understanding of the big ideas (Wiggins & McTighe, 1998). Grouping skills and knowledge into these categories helped the task force clarify priorities and determine where teacher professional development should be concentrated. The long-term outcomes for students are in the "deep understanding" category.

Each school's China committee will determine a tentative set of skills and knowledge it wants students to acquire during their years in that school. The CCC Task Force is not yet ready to propose a consistent pattern across schools. Rather than one set curriculum, it wants teachers to build on the student learning outcomes that seem most relevant at their grade level and that mesh with their interests.

Completing the AIM. The Inquiry Team produced a draft of the AIM that worked backward from the long-term student learning outcomes to the short-term outcomes and student learning experiences. Those on the team recognize that they did not identify specific content at this point but did identify instructors' practices. Based on the evaluative inquiry, they will specify content later, once teachers are more familiar with China. The Inquiry Team worked backward from the long-term outcomes for students to the outcomes and learning experiences for teachers. Next, as with student learning experiences, it identified instructional methods and will identify content later.

Next, the Inquiry Team filled in the characteristics of the system infrastructure it deemed most important to support the teaching and learning. It did not specify a certain combination of factors at this point but instead envisioned a situation where the factors collectively provide strong support for learning about China with no major resistance factors. The Inquiry Team realized the infrastructure must support much more than China in the curriculum. It developed the AIM shown in Figure 7.3.

The CCC Task Force views this vision (AIM) as tentative and anticipates that its vision may change as it obtains information from the evaluative inquiry.

80

Figure 7.3. Action and Inquiry Map for Sustainability Inquiry (students and teachers)

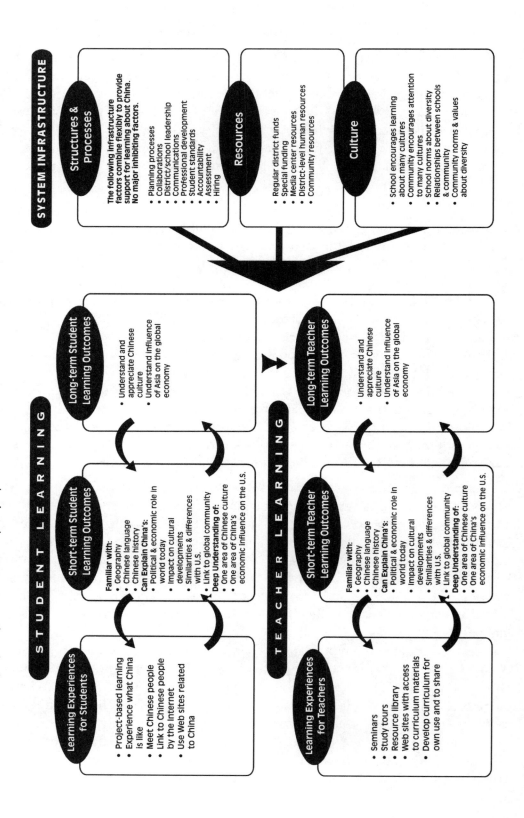

SYSTEM INFRASTRUCTURE

Structures & Processes

The following infrastructure factors combine flexibly to provide support for learning about China. **No major inhibiting factors.**

- Planning processes
- Collaborations
- District/school leadership
- Communications
- Professional development
- Student standards
- Accountability
- Assessment
- Hiring

Resources

- Regular district funds
- Special funding
- Media center resources
- District-level human resources
- Community resources

Culture

- School encourages learning about many cultures
- Community encourages attention to many cultures
- School norms about diversity
- Relationships between schools & community
- Community norms & values about diversity

STUDENT LEARNING

Long-term Student Learning Outcomes

- Understand and appreciate Chinese culture
- Understand influence of Asia on the global economy

Short-term Student Learning Outcomes

Familiar with:
- Geography
- Chinese language
- Chinese history

Can Explain China's:
- Political & economic role in world today
- Impact on cultural developments
- Similarities & differences with U.S.
- Link to global community

Deep Understanding of:
- One area of Chinese culture
- One area of China's economic influence on the U.S.

Learning Experiences for Students

- Project-based learning
- Experience what China is like
- Meet Chinese people
- Link to Chinese people by the Internet
- Use Web sites related to China

TEACHER LEARNING

Long-term Teacher Learning Outcomes

- Understand and appreciate Chinese culture
- Understand influence of Asia on the global economy

Short-term Teacher Learning Outcomes

Familiar with:
- Geography
- Chinese language
- Chinese history

Can Explain China's:
- Political & economic role in world today
- Impact on cultural developments
- Similarities & differences with U.S.
- Link to global community

Deep Understanding of:
- One area of Chinese culture
- One area of China's economic influence on the U.S.

Learning Experiences for Teachers

- Seminars
- Study tours
- Resource library
- Web sites with access to curriculum materials
- Develop curriculum for own use and to share

Planning the Sustainability Inquiry

Chapter Overview

When planning a Sustainability inquiry you look at three separate but related components: (a) student learning, (b) teacher learning, and (c) the infrastructure. The approach becomes manageable when you think in terms of developing an inquiry for each of the components with links between components and the desired results for students.

You develop task and timeline charts for data collection, analysis, synthesis, and communications, select the Inquiry Team, and consider budgetary issues. The pattern is similar to that in the Quality inquiry design but is complicated by having three components instead of one or two.

This chapter describes how Clark Community School District's temporary Inquiry Team developed its plan. It covers how the team defined the syntheses and analyses that guided the inquiry work. After approval of these by the CCC Task

Force, the Inquiry Team developed the budget, tasks, and timelines for data collection, analysis, and synthesis as well as communications to the Task Force and other users. The chapter ends with appointment of the ongoing Inquiry Team to carry out the inquiry work.

Identifying Inquiry Users

The first issue in planning an evaluative inquiry is determining who will use the results. As we saw in Chapter 7, Clark Community School District initially started to discuss the inquiry before it had plans in place for a defind China initiative. This was because Joseph, a middle school social studies teacher, had been part of an inquiry process at Summit and thus recognized early on that the rumblings of support for a China-related initiative should be grounded in an accompanying evaluative inquiry. When questioned by Esther (the inquiry coach), Joseph speculated that the users would be "those of us who want to bring China into the curriculum. We want to figure out how to be sure our efforts are not wasted. I think we are interested in both the quality of the content now being taught and the infrastructure that supports it."

Esther agreed that enthusiastic teachers were critical to success, but she wanted an identified initiative in place with designated decision makers before starting an evaluative inquiry: "I'm nervous about designing an inquiry without knowing whether the [informal group has] the decision-making power to use the results." At that stage in their discussions, the district curriculum director became involved and the CCC Task Force was born. This Task Force will be the primary user, with teachers throughout the school district, administrators, policymakers, community members, and parents as secondary users. Christine invited three people—Lu Fan (the district research director), Joseph, and Ricardo (a principal)—to serve as the temporary Inquiry Team.

Defining Syntheses and Analyses

The CCC Task Force's AIM provides the framework for the Vision-Action and Next Steps Syntheses. In effect, the syntheses say that the Task Force wants to understand how current activities match the vision expressed in the AIM and what next steps are appropriate to move toward the vision.

Inquiry Components

To organize the data collection and analyses, the temporary Inquiry Team divided the inquiry into three components—student learning, teacher learning, and infrastructure.

Student Learning

Recognizing that the schools were not yet ready to measure student outcomes on the China-related curriculum, the temporary Inquiry Team decided to start by asking the newly appointed China Committee at each school to determine whether the existing China-related curriculum is linked to the two long-term student learning outcomes proposed by the CCC Task Force. The committees will determine what China-related short- and long-term student learning outcomes are being addressed at the school, how well the curriculum materials used to teach about China are focused on the learning outcomes, and whether teachers have assessments of student learning related to the learning outcomes.

This activity constitutes a rudimentary inquiry into program quality. It positions the schools to undertake a more thorough Quality inquiry in the future. Joseph (the teacher with past inquiry experience) served as the coach for the school teams. Esther and Joseph developed a simple survey to help the committees gather the necessary information. Each school's China committee summarized the data and provided it to the cross-school China Inquiry Team for inclusion in its syntheses.

Teacher Learning

The China Consortium, providers of professional development for teachers, will handle the inquiry of teacher learning. They already have an evaluation team consisting of representatives from several districts who participate in the cross-district professional development. Clark Community School District requested information from this group about the extent to which the professional development the Consortium provides for teachers matches the district's long-term student learning outcomes. The Inquiry Team will include the results in its syntheses.

The rudimentary analyses of the student and teacher learning components of the AIM, along with the more intensive look at the infrastructure, will serve as the basis for the Inquiry Team to suggest the next steps for the initiative.

Infrastructure

The district's cross-school Inquiry Team will focus its work on the infrastructure. It wants to identify the infrastructure factors that most influence teaching and learning about China. The remainder of the discussion about Clark Community's inquiry planning is restricted to the infrastructure focus.

Infrastructure Analyses

I find two analyses particularly helpful when investigating the infrastructure. These two analyses, Change Forces and Historical Patterns, with their accompanying questions, usually capture the important insights about the infrastructure. The results of these analyses lead to the Vision-Action and Next Steps Syntheses for the users.

Change Forces Analysis

The Change Forces analysis answers the question: What are the forces for and against the change that will be brought about by the initiative? The Change Forces analysis provides a means to summarize data from questionnaires, interviews, document reviews, focus groups, or other means of collecting data.

Historical Patterns Analysis

The Historical Patterns analysis answers the question "What do the changes in the community and schools over the past 40 years imply for our future changes?"

This analysis is designed to discover long-term trends in a community or school and to determine the implications of these trends for future work.

I explain both of these analyses in Chapter 9.

Clark Community Example

The CCC Task Force told the temporary Inquiry Team that it was mainly interested in knowing what changes in the infrastructure might be needed to support the two long-term learning outcomes for students: (a) that all students will understand and appreciate Chinese culture and (b) that all students will understand the influence of Asia on the global economy. It also wanted to know if the vision, including the strategy for reaching the outcomes, seemed appropriate for the district. The CCC Task Force translated this request into the following questions:

- To what extent does the actual situation in Clark Community School District match our vision of student learning about China?
- How might we adjust our infrastructure and/or our vision in the best interest of students' learning about China?
- What are promising next steps for strengthening the link between student and teacher learning experiences and the desired learning outcomes for students?

The temporary Inquiry Team concluded that it could answer these questions by preparing Vision-Action and Next Steps Syntheses based on both Change Forces and Historical Patterns analyses. These analyses would be complemented by the data from the schools' China committees about student learning and the China Consortium on the link of professional development activities to desired student learning outcomes.

Determining the Budget and Resources

The temporary Inquiry Team determined that teachers who joined the Inquiry Team could devote up to four days of time to the work. The amount of time available from community members was expected to vary widely. The district research director agreed to commit the time of a staff member in his department to the work. The district research director and Christine each committed two more days to the inquiry work.

Christine accessed a special budget for school renewal to support the time of Inquiry Team members. The time for teachers was already covered through another budget designated for task forces and professional development work. Some teachers who joined the Inquiry Team decided to take time during the regular school day and have substitutes in their classrooms while other teachers decided to work in the evenings or on weekends and be paid a stipend for the work.

Developing Tasks and Timeline Charts

The same charts used in the Quality evaluative inquiry are applicable to the Sustainability inquiry. In fact, these charts are highly generalizable to most evaluations.

Clark Example

The temporary Inquiry Team made a presentation to the CCC Task Force about its proposed tasks and timelines. Joseph posted a copy of the Task Force's vision as expressed through the AIM. The AIM showed how the three parts of the inquiry design fit with the three components of the vision. He explained how information would be collected about the student and teacher learning components of the AIM. Then he explained the analyses and data collected that focused on the infrastructure (see Table 8.1). Here is the substance of his remarks:

> **ANALYSIS OF CHANGE FORCES**
> We will gather data from district administrators, community members, students, and teachers to understand how the education system's structures, processes, resources, and culture support or inhibit achieving the desired China-related outcomes for students. We will do interviews with district administrators and a few teachers. We will survey a sample of teachers, students, and community members. We also will review district policy and other documents.
>
> **ANALYSIS OF HISTORICAL PATTERNS**
> We want to learn more about historical patterns of change in our district as well. We will do this by holding focus groups that include community members and educators. As you know, we have a culturally diverse community. Therefore, we want our focus groups to be culturally diverse. We want your ideas about how we might best configure the groups.
>
> We will collect the initial information by early March. We will conduct our analyses by early April and report back to you by mid-April. Then we will have time to communicate to our teachers and administrators in early May and to parents, business leaders, and the China Consortium in late May or early June. We hope the China Consortium can use the information to at least make a few adjustments in this summer's professional development activities if warranted.

Although those on the CCC Task Force asked a number of questions and had several refinements, they basically approved the plan. Next, Joseph explained the Inquiry Team's anticipated communications to the CCC Task Force, teachers in all the schools, administrators, parents, business leaders, and the China Consortium (see Table 8.2). With the plan in place, it was time to establish the ongoing Inquiry Team.

Table 8.1 Clark Community Schools' China Initiative (Sustainability example): Analysis and Data Collection Tasks and Timeline Chart

Analysis	Questions	Data Collection				
		Information Sources	Instruments	Time Frame	Who	Time
Infrastructure Change Forces	Which infrastructure and social forces are supporting and which are inhibiting bringing China into the curriculum? What are the best options for adjusting the infrastructure to bring China into the curriculum?	Selected district administrators and teachers	Interviews	March	Two IT members	4 hours
		District policy and other documents	Document review	March	Two IT members	4 hours
Historical Trends	What are the past relationships between community changes and school/curriculum changes?	Community members, students, teachers	Culture survey	March	Two IT members	8 hours
		Community members, educators	Focus groups	March	Three IT members	2 hours
Student Learning	Are learning experiences in the schools aligned with the desired student learning outcomes?	All teachers currently teaching about China	Survey	March	School committee	2 hours
Teacher Learning	Are the professional development activities for educators provided by the China Consortium aligned with the desired student learning outcomes?	China Consortium documents	Document review	March	China Consortium Evaluation Team	3 hours

Table 8.2 Clark Community School District's China Initiative Evaluative Inquiry: Tasks and Timeline Chart

Users	Methods	Time Frame	Messages
Clark Community China Task Force (CCC Task Force)	Inquiry Team (IT) meets with CCC Task Force; IT and CCC Task Force members meet with each school's China Committee	April 15	(Completed after syntheses are done)
Internal partners: • Clark Community teachers	• Representatives of IT, CCC Task Force, and school's China Committee attend faculty meeting at each school • Chair of school's China Committee sends e-mail message to school's faculty summarizing messages and asks for feedback; orient toward summer professional development opportunites	May 15	
• District curriculum leaders and District Strategic Planning Committee	Representatives of IT and CCC Task Force meet with them	May 30	
External partners: • Parents • Business leaders	Article in local newspaper from district curriculum leader and IT and CCC Task Force chairs, including offer to speak to any groups or individuals about the work	June 6	
China Consortium	Meeting with China Consortium staff (focus on implications for summer professional development)		

Establishing the Inquiry Team

Because the work focuses on the infrastructure, it is important to include administrators as well as teachers on the team. It may also be appropriate to include community members. Make sure that you have the people necessary to carry out the data collection, analysis, synthesis, and sharing of results. Different people may be involved in different activities. Also consider whether you need a professional evaluator to serve as a coach or to develop instruments, collect data, and/or conduct analyses. Clark Community School District's Inquiry Team included teachers, administrators, and community members.

Data Collection and Analysis in the Sustainability Inquiry Design

Chapter Overview

This chapter explains how to collect data and conduct the Change Forces and the Historical Patterns analyses to determine the ability of the education system's infrastructure to support your initiative. The chapter is organized around the two analyses. Each analysis description begins with a general explanation followed by its application using the China initiative of the Clark Community School District. In the

Clark example, data are collected for these analyses using four tools. Interviews, document review, and a culture survey are used to look at change forces. Focus groups are used to understand historical patterns.

Change Forces Analysis

Purpose

The purpose of the Change Forces analysis is to develop a general idea of the strength and nature of the forces for and against the desired change, such as the school district's China initiative. Knowing roughly the strength of the change forces helps determine the next steps toward the vision. However, it is important to remember that situations are continually changing and unexpected forces can overwhelm those that seem important at a given point in time. The point here is not so much to determine exactly the balance of forces as to understand the dynamics of the forces of change and resistance. This information is valuable for developing a Sustainability strategy. By systematically looking at a wide range of factors, the Inquiry Team can bring insightful reflection to the analysis.

This analysis occurs in several steps leading up to the use of a grid showing four quadrants representing the strength of forces for and against the desired change (see Figure 9.1). Using the Change Forces grid, you can estimate the level and nature of change to expect and what factors are most useful to adjust to lead to sustainability (see Strebel, 1992).

Strebel's research showed that when both the change forces and the resistance forces are strong, disruptive change occurs (upper left quadrant of Figure 9.1). When resistance forces are strong and change forces are weak, there tends to be no change (lower left quadrant). When both change and resistance forces are relatively weak, change tends to be sporadic but does lead to gradual change (lower right quadrant). If the change forces are more intense but the resistance forces are still weak, a pattern of continuous change is likely to ensue (upper right quadrant). This is typically the most desirable situation.

With this as a background, let's look now at how to gather and summarize data to use for the Change Forces analysis.

Infrastructure Ratings

To conduct the Change Forces analysis, you will need a measure of the strength (either positive or negative) of the features of the infrastructure. In some situations, Inquiry Team members may have sufficient information themselves to immediately do a rating of forces for and against the initiative, but in most cases they will gather data from others. It is helpful for the Inquiry Team to have a common format to summarize their data. One method is to develop a rating and summary form based on the features of the infrastructure being investigated.

The Clark Community Inquiry Team developed a Change Forces Rating and Summary Form that easily can be adapted to other situations. The form (see page 92) should be accompanied by pages with space to write comments about the rated categories.

Collecting Data for the Change Forces Analysis

An Inquiry Team uses the rating scale to summarize data from multiple data collection activities and people. The data collection instruments are likely to be interviews, questionnaires, document review guides, focus groups, and/or observations. Each technique provides somewhat different information and has cost and other advantages and disadvantages depending on the situation (see Chapter 14 for references that provide details on data collection instruments).

Clark Example

The Inquiry Team gathered data for its Change Forces analysis through a combination of interviews, document review, and school and community questionnaires.

Figure 9.1. Change Forces Grid

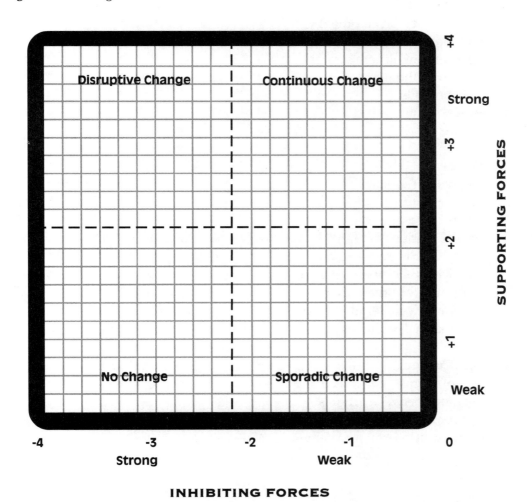

Change Forces Rating and Summary Form

Directions: Indicate the data source for your ratings and summary. Then rate the extent to which each listed factor supports or inhibits student learning about China.

Data Source(s) _____

	Strongly Inhibits				Neutral				Strongly Supports	
Structures and Processes										
a. District and school planning processes	-4	-3	-2	-1	0	1	2	3	4	NA
b. Collaborations	-4	-3	-2	-1	0	1	2	3	4	NA
c. Leadership	-4	-3	-2	-1	0	1	2	3	4	NA
d. Communication	-4	-3	-2	-1	0	1	2	3	4	NA
e. Curriculum	-4	-3	-2	-1	0	1	2	3	4	NA
f. Professional development methods/activities (teachers and administrators)	-4	-3	-2	-1	0	1	2	3	4	NA
g. Student standards	-4	-3	-2	-1	0	1	2	3	4	NA
h. Accountability	-4	-3	-2	-1	0	1	2	3	4	NA
i. Assessment	-4	-3	-2	-1	0	1	2	3	4	NA
j. Hiring	-4	-3	-2	-1	0	1	2	3	4	NA
Resources										
a. Financial resources: regular district funds	-4	-3	-2	-1	0	1	2	3	4	NA
b. Financial resources: special funds	-4	-3	-2	-1	0	1	2	3	4	NA
c. School media center resources	-4	-3	-2	-1	0	1	2	3	4	NA
d. District-level human resources	-4	-3	-2	-1	0	1	2	3	4	NA
e. Community human resources	-4	-3	-2	-1	0	1	2	3	4	NA
f. Community material and financial resources	-4	-3	-2	-1	0	1	2	3	4	NA
Climate/Culture										
a. School norms	-4	-3	-2	-1	0	1	2	3	4	NA
b. Relations between schools and community	-4	-3	-2	-1	0	1	2	3	4	NA
c. Community norms and values	-4	-3	-2	-1	0	1	2	3	4	NA

Interviews at Clark

Two Inquiry Team members worked together to interview three longtime district administrators who were very familiar with the structures, processes, resources, and culture of the district. They tape-recorded the interviews and took extensive notes in case the tape recording failed.

Two other Inquiry Team members interviewed three teachers who had been to China and were now teaching about China. Interviewees were asked to describe how the infrastructure factors identified on the AIM support student learning about Chinese culture and China's impact on the global economy.

After the tapes were transcribed, two retired social studies teachers reviewed the transcriptions. They organized the information according to the categories given on the rating scale and then developed codes for themes within the categories (see Glesne & Peshkin, 1992, for information on coding qualitative data). They organized the information separately for the teachers and the administrators so they could determine whether the two groups viewed the infrastructure factors differently.

After they had organized the information, they worked with the Inquiry Team members who had conducted the interviews. Together they reviewed the data and reached agreement on an overall rating of each characteristic for each interviewee. On the accompanying pages of the form, they summarized succinctly the major points that led to their ratings. They determined an average rating separately for the teacher interviewees and the administrator interviewees.

Document Review at Clark

Christine, her staff, and the human resources director gathered selected district policy documents and organized them in the conference room. Two Inquiry Team members reviewed the documents to determine whether district hiring, teacher evaluation, standards selection, and professional development supported or inhibited bringing China into the curriculum. They used the same summary and rating form used for interviews.

School and Community Culture Questionnaire

Two Inquiry Team members developed a simple one-page questionnaire to gather the views of students, teachers, and community members. The questionnaire asked people to rate the extent to which the community and schools are accepting and respectful of different cultures and the importance of students learning about different cultures, including the Asian culture. Questionnaires went to students (Grades 5 through 12) in one class in each school. Teachers completed the questionnaire at a faculty meeting. The Inquiry Team also distributed the survey to parents who attended the spring parent-teacher conferences. To make the survey accessible to as many parents as possible, a community member translated it into Spanish. The district provided translators to assist parents who spoke other languages.

Students in the high school computer class entered the data and calculated average scores for the survey using a computer software program they were learning. They calculated average scores for the group as a whole as well as separately for students, teachers, and parents. Then within each group, they calculated averages separately for the major ethnic groups in the community. The Inquiry Team was surprised to learn that students and parents viewed the school and community as much less open to diversity than the teachers had.

Conducting the Change Forces Analysis

Completing the Change Forces analysis involves three major steps.

Step 1: Consolidate and Rank Order the Ratings

If you have collected data from multiple sources or used multiple methods, you will have several summary rating forms. Average the ratings across sources but note in the explanation section of the form where the ratings from different sources are noticeably different. Another option is to not consolidate the data in these situations. For example, administrators may see the resources for a particular effort as adequate while teachers do not; different ethnic groups may view the openness of the school to the community differently; teachers may think the school is more inviting than students or parents do.

Once you have consolidated the ratings, select the infrastructure characteristics with ratings higher than .5. Make a list of them in rank order, with the most supportive at the top. Now make a list of the infrastructure characteristics that have a rating less than -.5. Put them in rank order, with the most inhibiting at the bottom of the list. List the average rating for each factor. Then calculate the average of the averages in the supporting category. Do the same for those in the inhibiting category. These two ratings together identify coordinates on the Change Forces grid if you did not weight the relative importance of the factors. You may prefer to weight factors differently. This will affect the average ratings.

See the list of supporting and inhibiting factors prepared by members of the Clark Inquiry Team on the next page.

Step 2: Work With the Change Forces Grid

The next step in the process is to convene the Inquiry Team to analyze the results in relation to the Change Forces grid. It is helpful to have a large wall chart of the grid in Figure 9.1. As a starting point for the discussion, list the supporting factors along the right hand side of the grid approximately in line with their average ratings. List the inhibiting factors along the bottom of the grid, placed according to their average ratings. The visual display of the position of the forces facilitates conversation. You might want to put the factors on sticky notes that can be moved around. For example, during the discussion you may want to display how you would like the factors to be positioned a year from now.

Next, identify the position on the grid represented by the average ratings on inhibiting and supporting factors as determined by the calculations in Step 1. In the

Supporting Factors   **Average Ratings**

Supporting Factors	Average Ratings
China Consortium collaboration	3.5
China Consortium professional development	3.5
District/school leadership	3.5
Special funds	3.0
School norms (teacher views)	2.0

Average of Supporting Factors   **3.1**

Inhibiting Factors

Inhibiting Factors	Average Ratings
Planning processes	-1.0
Accountability	-1.3
School/community relations	-1.5
Community norms	-1.5
Regular district funds	-2.5
School norms (student, parent views)	-3.2
Student standards	-3.5
Media center resources	-3.5
State assessment	-3.8

Average of Inhibiting Factors   **-2.4**

case of the Clark schools, the average rating of the supporting factors was 3.1. The average for the inhibiting factors was 2.4. By locating the position on the grid using these two coordinates (-2.4, 3.1), you find that the initiative is positioned in the disruptive change quadrant slightly over the border from the continuous change quadrant.

Let me remind you again that this is not an exact science. Rather, this positioning gives you a rough idea of the situation. It is designed to stimulate conversation about what changes among all of the factors are likely to be the most helpful in achieving continuous change. For example, in the Clark Community School District situation, the state assessments were rated as a very inhibiting factor. They are important to the community, yet they heavily emphasize basic skills and do not address knowledge of China. The district may have little influence over the assessments. Instead of trying to change the assessments, the CCC Task Force may want to develop assessments of their own regarding China that balance the effects of these assessments and give students, educators, and the community a broader picture of student learning than what is represented on the state assessments.

At the meeting, give each participant a list of the supporting and inhibiting factors as well as the rating form used to summarize results. Have each subgroup that gathered and analyzed data give a short oral summary of its major findings related to the features. As the team members listen to and participate in the discussion, they seek to understand the overall balance of the many factors and what adjustments could be made in them. They discuss which features of the infrastructure seem to be most open to adjustment by the CCC Task Force or others.

Step 3: Choose a Strategy

In the final step, your team considers the implications of the initiative's location on the grid and the nature of the forces affecting it. This discussion produces ideas for the Next Steps Synthesis. In doing so, here are some considerations based on Strebel's (1992) research about intervention approaches that effective organizational leaders use in different situations.

If the change forces are declining or low and resistors are closed to change (the "no change" quadrant), it is best to not try to make changes in the organization as a whole. Changes are best done through a separate group that is protected from the forces of the status quo. Outsiders are likely to find it futile to encourage change in the organization as a whole.

If the organization tends to be in the quadrant of "sporadic change," where change forces are declining or low and resistance is low, the strategy tends to be one of incremental targeted change. Partnerships and alliances specific to a particular targeted change are important in this situation.

If the organization tends to be in the "continuous change" quadrant, where change forces are strong and growing and resistors are open to change, an ongoing revitalization strategy is more possible. It involves long-term investment in incorporating a change (such as bringing China into the curriculum) with slow continuous adaptation to changing conditions.

If an organization is in the "disruptive change" quadrant, where change forces are strong and growing and resistors are closed to change, significant restructuring of the organization is likely to be the mechanism for handling the situation. If the analysis shows that an initiative such as incorporating China into the curriculum is likely to lead to disruptive change, the group would need to weigh carefully if the initiative is worth the cost of major organizational restructuring. Instead, the group may recommend that the initiative be slowed down until certain factors can be adjusted to move the initiative into the continuous or sporadic change quadrants.

With this general information in mind, the team considers steps the initiative leaders might take to reduce key resistant forces and/or adjust certain supportive forces so the work can move into the area of "continuous change" or at least "sporadic change." The continuous change area is the one where the change is likely to be sustained long term. If it does not seem feasible to move an initiative initially placed in the "no change" or "disruptive change" quadrants into one of the other quadrants, it is risky to proceed.

Clark Example

Once Clark's Inquiry Team positioned the district on the grid, it knew what inhibiting factors needed to be reduced or dampened to move them into the continuous change quadrant. The Inquiry Team also recognized that its current positioning close to the continuous change category was very dependent on its connection with one outside organization. If team members wanted to be comfortably in the continuous change category, they would need to increase factors that better connected their work to the community and to the regular funding of the district. They concluded that the most problematic force was the community's strong attention to the state standards and assessments that ignored China. Then they saw this as an opportunity. They could build on the community's interest in student assessment by creating their own assessment of student learning about China to report alongside state assessments. In fact, they could make the assessment of learning about China even more appealing than the state assessments.

The factor that the Inquiry Team felt the CCC Task Force could influence most quickly was the media center resources. It knew the China Consortium would help the schools obtain such resources. It identified school and community norms as fundamental factors that it needed to start working on as soon as possible. It may take a long time to change these factors, but unless they change, the initiative will always be facing an uphill battle.

Before the Inquiry Team went any further on drawing implications for the Next Steps synthesis, it decided it would wait until it had the results from the Historical Patterns analysis. Those on the team also needed some time to think about additional ways to leverage the factors they had investigated to support the initiative.

The Historical Patterns Analysis

The purpose of this analysis is to obtain a historical view of the dynamics that may be affecting a school or district's ability to change. The process identifies influences on the education system that may only be evident when a longer period of time is considered. Due to frequent changes in leadership within schools, "institutional memory" is often lost. This analysis restores a historical perspective.

Data collection and analysis are meshed for the Historical Patterns analysis. A focus group process is used. Focus group attendees should include people who collectively can depict the history of the school and community for about the past 40 years. Retired teachers and administrators as well as practicing educators are needed. Involve community members from different socioeconomic and ethnic groups with varying lengths of time in the community. The sessions are usually very enjoyable and beneficial for participants. Long-time residents and educators have a chance to share their history and newcomers are intrigued by the past.

When focus group participants enter the room, they see a 5-by-8-foot paper chart covering the entire wall. It is blank except for labels across the top for the decades to be considered (such as from 1960 to 2000) and three rows labeled "external forces," "internal forces," and "curriculum changes." The labels reflect the questions being addressed, namely "What have been the major external forces that have shaped our community and schools over the past 40 years?" "What have been the major internal forces that have shaped our community and schools over the past 40 years?" and "What curriculum changes have occurred in our schools over the past 40 years?" By the time the group finishes, the chart is filled with colored sticky notes with answers to the questions.

After the introduction and an explanation of the purpose and process of the session, the facilitator asks each person to write brief answers to the questions. Each answer is on a separate sticky note. The participants post their notes on the chart under the appropriate decade and in the appropriate row. The facilitator may also ask people to put a "+" by forces they believe to be positive and encourage change, a "−" by those that are negative and/or inhibit change, and a "0" by those they feel are neutral.

After the notes are posted, the facilitator invites people to peruse the charts, considering what others have written. With everyone seated again, the facilitator opens a discussion of the forces of change in each decade. As people talk, two members of the Inquiry Team listen for themes that surface. For example, themes may be that curriculum changes are initiated by state policy, financial issues, changes in the ethnic makeup of the community, strong teacher leaders, or professional development events. At least two other Inquiry Team members take notes and use a tape recorder.

The group takes a break while the Inquiry Team members who listened for themes arrange the sticky notes to reduce duplication and highlight themes. They keep the sticky notes in the correct time period and related to the appropriate questions. To close the session, the Inquiry Team members who listened for themes review with the group what they identified and ask the group for reactions.

Following the meeting, Inquiry Team members review all information and construct a timeline of key forces and events that have shaped the school's history and note the related curriculum changes. In addition to the chronological view, they write a summary of the key forces and how they have affected the school. They especially note negative ones that are likely to be repeated if there is no intervention.

Clark Example

The Inquiry Team at Clark used the process given above. The Inquiry Team invited several retired teachers and administrators as well as several practicing teachers and administrators who had been in the schools for 10 or more years. Business owners, religious and community leaders, social service agency staff, and long-time residents also participated. They sought out people representing different ethnic and socioeconomic groups in the community. Collectively, attendees of the focus group displayed a rich knowledge of the history of the school and community over the past 40 years. The recorders taped the discussion and took extensive notes.

Rather than have everyone attend at once, the Inquiry Team held a "rolling" focus group over the course of an afternoon and evening. People were invited to attend any 1.5-hour block of time with a half-hour break before the start of the next session. For each group, the facilitator briefly described what information was already on the chart and asked the new group to add factors or emphasize ones they thought were particularly important.

The Inquiry Team learned from the analysis that the curriculum changed very slowly over the years. When it did finally change, it was usually in response to state policies that mandated change. Sometimes, it was driven by special professional development opportunities for teachers. The curriculum did not adjust as the demographics of the community changed. The Inquiry Team members were surprised. They thought the school and the community were more in touch with the social context and were making their own decisions.

Synthesizing and Communicating Results From a Sustainability Inquiry

Chapter Overview

This chapter addresses the synthesis and communication of results from a Sustainability evaluative inquiry. It presents the Vision-Action and Next Steps Syntheses conducted by the Clark Community School District's Inquiry Team, how the Team shared the results with the CCC Task Force, and how the Task Force communicated the results to other educators in the schools and to the community.

The general processes for synthesizing and communicating the results are the same in the Sustainability as in the Quality inquiry design. However, the Sustainability design has more categories in its Action and Inquiry Map and thus the syntheses are a bit more complex.

The Vision-Action Synthesis

In mid-January, the Inquiry Team met to conduct its Vision-Action Synthesis. It was time to step back and look at the situation as a whole.

There was a large version of the CCC Task Force's AIM on the wall (see Figure 7.3). Next to it was a blank version of the AIM labeled "Current Action." The Inquiry Team members' first task was to fill in information about the current situation so they could contrast it with the AIM. They began with the Student Learning boxes to reground themselves in the purpose for looking at the infrastructure. They described the current Student Learning situation based on information gathered from the China committees in the schools. They did the same for the Teacher Learning boxes based on information from the China Consortium's evaluation team. Finally, they described the current infrastructure features, using the information from the Change Forces and Historical Patterns analyses they had conducted.

Student Learning

The Inquiry Team first considered the Long-Term Student Outcomes box on the current action chart. The data showed that the schools had no long-term outcomes specific to China. Two schools had a stated outcome that their students would understand and appreciate cultural diversity. The team included this information on the chart.

Next, those on the Inquiry Team filled in the box for Learning Experiences available to students—a fourth-grade geography unit, a sixth-grade ancient history unit, a tenth-grade world history course with attention to China from 1900 to 1950, and an elective Asian Studies class at the high school. The CCC Task Force had specified in its vision of students' learning experiences that students would undertake projects about China; meet Chinese people in person or through the Internet; experience what China is like; and use Web sites related to China. Instead, those on the Task Force found that most teaching about China was textbook driven with little hands-on work. The data showed that elementary and middle school classrooms had few maps of China or artifacts that made China real to the students.

The Short-Term Learning Outcomes for the fourth-, sixth-, and tenth-grade units included students' being familiar with China's geography and history, explaining China's impact on cultural developments, and explaining differences from and similarities with the United States. The elective Asian Studies course at the high school had outcomes partially congruent with the CCC Task Force's vision; students were expected to explain China's impact on cultural developments and differences from and similarities with the United States. However, the course included very little about China's political and economic role in the world today.

Overall, the CCC Task Force found no learning outcomes related to several areas it had envisioned—Chinese language, deep understanding about China, or China's political and economic role in the world today.

Teacher Learning

The information from the China Consortium showed that the long- and short-term learning outcomes and learning experiences provided for teachers were congruent with those in the CCC Task Force's AIM. Teachers would need to engage in many professional development opportunities to address all of the short-term learning outcomes. It would likely take a teacher three to five years of involvement to address them all.

Infrastructure

On the Current Action chart, the Inquiry Team addressed the infrastructure factors. It rank-ordered them within each category (Structures/Process, Resources, and Culture) to move from the most to least supportive. The Inquiry Team highlighted in green the two most supportive Structures/Processes (leadership, collaboration with the China Consortium) and in red the most inhibiting (assessment). It highlighted "special funding" in green and "regular district funding" in red in the Resources box. In the Culture box, it highlighted nothing in green and "relationships between schools and community" and "community norms and values about diversity" in red.

Summary

While others were taking a break before doing the Next Steps Synthesis, one Inquiry Team member used his laptop to prepare a one-page summary of the differences between the current action and the Task Force's vision based on the displays on the wall. He agreed to send it by e-mail to the rest of the team members so they could suggest changes before it was used at the CCC Task Force meeting in a couple of weeks.

The Next Steps Synthesis

In preparation for the Next Steps Synthesis, the Inquiry Team posted its Change Forces analysis chart and Historical Patterns chart on the wall along with the Vision-Action Synthesis. Each person on the team took 10 minutes to wander around viewing the displays and making notes about possible next steps. All wrote each suggestion on a separate sticky note and posted it on another wall under one of three labels: Student Learning, Teacher Learning, and Infrastructure. The team then broke into three groups. Each group reviewed one of the categories and identified what it considered the most important next steps based on the data. The full group reviewed the collective set of suggestions, looking for ways to build areas of concentrated focus and synergistic action among components of the AIM to sustain the China-related work.

The Inquiry Team summarized its Next Steps suggestions for the CCC Task Force as follows:

1. Build around the existing units and courses about China. Modify them to focus on the desired long- and short-term learning outcomes in a more comprehensive way. Encourage the teaching techniques envisioned by the CCC Task Force.

2. Develop two-year blocks of emphasis on China, such as Grades 3-4, 6-7, and 9-10, to help students connect their learning about China over time. Use demonstrations of student learning as the basis for connecting to the community.

3. Institute a yearly public exhibition of learning about China that both serves as an assessment of student learning and brings the community into the schools or the schools into the community. Use the exhibition as a balance to the state assessments.

4. Give teachers at the grade levels emphasizing China first priority for participating in professional development through the China Consortium. Work with the Consortium to tailor the professional development to help revise the curriculum, sharpen the focus on the desired outcomes, identify materials for the school media centers, and generate effective ways for students to demonstrate their learning.

5. Work with the district strategic planning committee to build a better relationship with the community concerning cultural diversity. Use the focus on China as a pilot approach for greater and more coherent emphases in the curriculum on non-European cultures.

6. Work with the administration and possibly the school board to develop a more secure funding base for professional development related to China as well as other cultures.

7. Continue the CCC Task Force and evaluative inquiry. Position the continued evaluative inquiry to also help the district strategic planning committee address the broader issues of cultural diversity.

An Inquiry Team member recorded the Next Steps suggestions and circulated them via e-mail to the rest of the team for final comment.

Before concluding the meeting, the Inquiry Team took 15 minutes to review its Tasks and Timeline for Communicating Results (see Figure 8.2) and confirmed its original plan to communicate with the CCC Task Force through a meeting. However, those on the Inquiry Team felt that the approach for communicating with others should be worked out with the CCC Task Force. They identified their most important messages:

1. Significant discrepancies exist between the Task Force's vision for student learning regarding China and current activities.

2. A promising multiyear strategy exists to support student and teacher learning about China. (Different features of the strategy would be emphasized with different user groups.)

3. The strategy can serve as an example for schools to increase the emphasis on diverse cultures.

Communicating Inquiry Results

Here is how the Clark Inquiry Team first communicated with the CCC Task Force and worked with it to communicate to others.

Communicating to the Action Team

The Inquiry Team met with the CCC Task Force and put the charts from its syntheses on the wall. It then placed the CCC Task Force's AIM (the vision) on the right-hand side of the front wall and the Current Action chart about five feet to its left. The Inquiry Team placed the Change Forces analysis and the Historical Patterns analysis charts on two other walls.

The Inquiry Team first reviewed the differences between the AIM and current actions. After clarification questions, it discussed the Change Forces and Historical Patterns analyses and then moved on to suggested Next Steps. The Inquiry Team had written its seven suggestions on seven footprints to place between the "action" and "vision" charts on the front wall. It concluded the presentation by distributing a one-page summary organized around the messages it wanted to emphasize. During and following supper, members of the Inquiry Team mingled with members of the Task Force members. They wandered around the room looking at the information of most interest to them. One member of the Inquiry Team stayed close to each of the displays to ensure that someone was available to answer questions.

The group reconvened in 45 minutes. The CCC Task Force chair led the meeting, asking the Task Force members for their reactions to the presentation. The reactions were generally positive. However, they decided they would not make a firm decision about the next steps yet. They would give people time to consider the ideas and generate additional or different ones. At its meeting the following week, the CCC Task Force would make decisions about its recommendations to the administration and would determine the main messages and means to communicate with other groups internal and external to the schools.

At its next meeting, the CCC Task Force confirmed the suggested next steps proposed by the Inquiry Team, with minor modifications.

Communicating With School and District Partners

Because the China initiative cut across the whole district, a number of groups needed information about the results of the inquiry. The CCC Task Force confirmed the original communications plan (see Figure 8.2) to use the schools' China committees as the means of reaching the faculty in each school and held a meeting for members of the school China committees.

At this meeting, the Inquiry Team repeated the presentation it had made to the CCC Task Force and gave the committees a one-page summary of the inquiry findings. The CCC Task Force discussed the suggested next steps with the school committees and obtained their input. It also gave the committees information about summer professional development available through the China Consortium. The committees shared the inquiry results with their faculty and provided feedback to the CCC Task Force by the end of the school year. They also shared information about the summer sessions conducted by the China Consortium, emphasizing those most relevant to their school and the proposed next steps from the CCC Task Force.

During the summer, the CCC Task Force and Inquiry Team chairs met with the district curriculum leaders and strategic planning committee to discuss the inquiry findings and feedback from the CCC Task Force and school committees. They determined what communications were needed with the superintendent and school board before communicating with the community at large.

Communicating With the Community

The Task Force expects to be ready in the fall to put an article in the local newspaper to start communications with parents, community members, and business leaders about the China initiative and their overall strategy based on the evaluative inquiry. They plan to use the key messages identified by the Inquiry Team but tailor the discussion of the strategy to those features that address the community's involvement. The article will include opportunities for the community to give feedback on the plan, interact with the CCC Task Force, and be part of the work next year.

The Next Steps of Evaluative Inquiry

In the fall, the CCC Task Force and Strategic Planning Committee decided to work together to plan the next phase of the evaluative inquiry. They decided to add one or more community members to the Inquiry Team. They began the fall with a renewed commitment to their mission and excitement about the strategy ahead. Although it would be a considerable amount of work, it would be meaningful and fruitful.

Part 3

Cultivation

I n Part 3, I describe how to inquire into the cultivation of an initiative beyond the first group of teachers or projects that begins the work. Cultivation becomes the focus after you have a process in place to monitor the quality of specific programs and the sustaining nature of the infrastructure. It is important to understand the basic elements of the initiative and its potential before expanding it. Cultivation reaches deep into the underlying philosophy of the school and the interplay among all aspects of teaching, learning, and the system's infrastructure. I use the situation of expanding a whole school change initiative at the hypothetical Winding Trail High School to illustrate the design (see the description below).

Chapter 11 looks at how to *position* the inquiry in relation to the initiative. Chapter 12 explains how to *plan* the Cultivation inquiry. As in the other two designs, planning begins with the intention to present two syntheses—Vision-Action and Next Steps—to the Action Team, but this time the syntheses are oriented around cultivation. Consequently, the content of these syntheses draws on different analyses, which in turn draw on different types of data collection. In Chapter 13, I explain the *data collection* as well as the *analyses and syntheses* that support insightful *communication* about the inquiry results to those responsible for the initiative.

Setting: Winding Trail High School

The Initiative: Whole School Change

For the past five years, Winding Trail High School has been redesigning itself toward a vision of high levels of learning for all students and teachers across all disciplines and changes in the infrastructure of the school. Those at Winding Trail are seeking to operate according to a vision based on eight guiding principles that encourage all students to achieve high levels of meaningful learning and the school to operate on explicitly democratic principles. A key guiding principle is changing the philosophy of education from teacher as deliverer of information with passive student roles to student-as-worker and teacher-as-coach.

Time Period for the Evaluative Inquiry

Last year, the Inquiry Team realized the results it had from its work to date using the Quality and Sustainability inquiry designs were not addressing important issues about the cultivation of the renewal beyond a limited group. At that time, the Inquiry Team began its Cultivation inquiry. Now it wants to go to a deeper level of investigation as it prepares for its accreditation self-study. Between October and January, the Inquiry Team plans the additional features of its Cultivation inquiry; gathers, analyzes and synthesizes data; discusses these with the School Renewal Committee; and prepares an additional section of its report for a February meeting with the accreditation review team. Following the accreditation visit, the Inquiry Team will share inquiry results with other parties involved in the work.

Demographics

Number of students: 1,108 in Grades 9-12

Ethnic breakdown: 71% Caucasion, 28% Hispanic, 1% other

Number of teachers: 60

Average years of teaching experience: 15

Average years at Winding Trail: 11

District enrollment: 15,160 (8% increase in the past year)

Community: Blue-collar suburb of large metropolitan area
    in the western United States

Context

Inquiry and Change Practices

The school has a School Renewal Committee that guides the whole school change. An Inquiry Team has been engaged in evaluative inquiry for several years using the Quality and Sustainability designs.

Teachers

Winding Trail has a number of innovative teachers scattered throughout the school who are eager to make changes. However, the school also has a large number of teachers who may intellectually agree with the guiding principles but are not sure how to put them into practice.

Administrative Practices

The principal and other school administrators strongly encourage teacher leadership and professional development.

The Players

The people named in the Winding Trail scenario are Jim, Kelly, and Roy, all of them teachers and Inquiry Team members.

11

Positioning the Cultivation Evaluative Inquiry

Chapter Overview

The Cultivation inquiry design is used for large-scale changes such as whole school change initiatives that involve many people and a philosophical shift in the approach to teaching, learning, and governance. Because it is used after a school has established a Quality or a Sustainability inquiry process, the inquiry users typically are already defined and no temporary Inquiry Team is needed. However, if you decide to use a temporary team, follow the same procedure used with the other two designs.

The major task in positioning a Cultivation inquiry is developing an elaborated version of the AIM used in the Sustainability design. The elaborated AIM shows change over time. In this chapter, I focus on the development of the AIM for the Cultivation design, illustrating it with the Winding Trail scenario. To set the stage for understanding the rationale behind the elaborated AIM, I first give background on Winding Trail's situation.

The Winding Trail High School Situation

Guiding Principles

Winding Trail has eight guiding principles. These roughly adhere to the common principles of the Coalition of Essential Schools but also contain ideas from other school reform efforts (see sidebar).

Through the guiding principles, Winding Trail expresses its intent to nurture meaningful, coherent learning rather than unconnected, discipline-based learning. Those involved want this relatively large school to have a personal, trusting, democratic, and caring culture.

Quality Focus

The Winding Trail Inquiry Team is pleased with its progress on studying the quality of student and teacher learning. Charts on department office walls show trends in student learning within the department over the past three years. The measures of student learning include grades, end-of-year exhibitions, culminating exhibitions for seniors, Advanced Placement test results, district and state assessments, and course failure rates. Other indirect measures of interest in learning include attendance, number of students taking Advanced Placement courses, and number of students who major in a discipline in college.

Winding Trail High School Guiding Philosophy

(Adapted from the common principles of the Coalition of Essential Schools. See www.essentialschools.org)

1. The school focuses on helping young people learn to use their minds well.
2. Each student masters a limited number of essential and meaningful skills and areas of knowledge that students need for living in a global society.
3. The student learning goals apply to all students. The means to these goals are personalized.
4. The dominant teaching and learning relationship is student-as-worker, teacher-as-coach.
5. Learning is assessed with tools based on students' performance of real tasks. Students exhibit their expertise before their family, community, teachers, and other students.
6. The culture of the school expresses caring, trust, decency, collaboration, and democratic practices.
7. The principal and teachers are committed not only to their discipline and students but also to the entire school and community.
8. The school honors diversity and models democratic practices.

Whenever Winding Trail makes an intentional change expected to affect one or more of these indicators, the Inquiry Team places a symbol along the trend line for these indicators and then watches to see if the trends change. Similarly, teachers make links between changes they make within courses and student achievement in the course. For example, two years ago, all teachers were required to identify and put into writing learning outcomes and assessments for each course they taught. Parents and students received a copy of the new higher expectations for each course. As part of the evaluative inquiry, Winding Trail studied the impact of this decision. Because the school had already been collecting data on the number of students who failed one or more courses each quarter, the Inquiry Team was able to compare the previous results with those of the new practice. Generally, it found that the failure rate jumped significantly in the first quarter of implementation and then returned to close to its previous level. This pattern reassured the school's Inquiry Team that students could meet higher expectations.

Sustainability Focus

The Winding Trail Inquiry Team also has looked at the school's infrastructure to see what structures, processes, resources, and culture issues might significantly affect the sustainability of its work. The Inquiry Team found several policies and processes that needed to be adjusted. For example, as a result of the inquiry, the district and the teachers' association negotiated for more professional development and planning time for teachers.

The Inquiry Team also conducted surveys, such as a periodic culture survey from the perspective of teachers and administrators. It gathered information on collaboration, decision making, leadership, and the openness of the environment and has been pleased to see patterns of change over time—in the right direction.

The findings from the inquiry go to the School Renewal Committee and then to the faculty through department meetings and newsletters; to students through student council; and to parents and community members through articles in the local newspaper. The school feels fortunate to have built a relationship with the newspaper that has endured through three different education editors in the past five years. The education editor comes to the school on a yearly basis to discuss education issues and the changes that are occurring.

Cultivation Focus

Last year, Winding Trail began to acknowledge that, although it could sustain a small pocket of change for a long time, it hadn't been able to expand the scope of the change beyond a certain group of teachers. So its Inquiry Team began a Cultivation inquiry into how the philosophy was being infused in the school and to understand the nature of the cultivation (or lack of cultivation) of the ideas beyond the small group of teachers actively practicing the new philosophy.

The AIM as a Continuum of Change

It generally takes a long time for a school to be transformed from one fundamental set of beliefs about education to another. The shift often involves changes in beliefs about teaching and learning as well as relationships (see the chart below).

Philosophical Approaches of School Systems

Old Philosophy	New Philosophy
Predominance of hierarchical decision making and rules orientation	Predominance of shared, collaborative decision making
Teacher as deliverer of information	Teacher as coach
Student as passive recipient	Student as worker
One-size-fits-all approach	Personalization
Abstract and procedural learning	Meaningful, real-life, project-based learning
Environment of control, threats for violating rules	Safe, supportive, respectful environment

To implement learning-focused changes, it is necessary to rethink all functions, practices, and policies of the school from the perspective of the new philosophy. A more elaborated AIM helps track indicators of the changes and the extent to which adoption has moved from a small group of people to become the school norm.

The elaborated AIM builds on the tendency of school transformation to occur in stages (see Figure 11.1).

Setting Up the Expanded AIM

The expanded AIM uses the stages of change shown in Figure 11.1 and the components of change shown in the Sustainability AIM. It is portrayed as a matrix (see Figure 11.2). Although actual change is not linear, it helps to picture the tasks within a framework so that you can track your progress. For the heading of each row, you choose a "component of change." The label is drawn from the categories in the Sustainability AIM (e.g., Resources). For the heading of each column, you will choose a label that represents one of the "phases of change" (e.g., Transition). The descriptors of the phases of change are not inflexible but, rather, are hazy indicators of the progression. Before looking at how to fill in the details on this matrix, here is some background on the components of change and phases of change.

Components of Change

In the matrix worksheet (Figure 11.2), I basically use the categories of a Sustainability AIM as the components of change (see Figure 7.1.) Recall that the Sustainability AIM had three sections—Student Learning, Teacher Learning, and Infrastructure. Both the student and teacher learning sections showed a linkage

Figure 11.1. Phases of Change

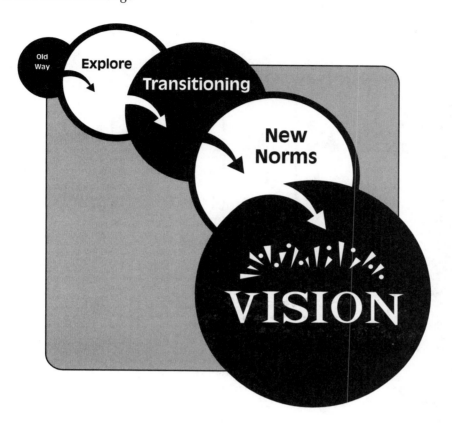

between learning experiences and outcomes. Additionally, the Teacher Learning Outcomes were determined by the Student Learning Outcomes. The Infrastructure was divided into the categories Structures/Processes, Resources, and Culture. For the Cultivation AIM, I divide the student learning section into Student Learning Outcomes and Learning Experiences for Students. I want to keep the emphasis on student learning because it drives the rest of the continuum. Thus I have listed it first. I do not subdivide the Teacher Learning component because the Student Learning Outcomes (row 1 in the matrix) also drives teacher learning. I keep the three sections of the system infrastructure—Structures/Processes, Resources, and Climate—separate.

You may find it useful to divide the Teacher Learning section into more parts or to collapse the Infrastructure components. As you work with such continua, you'll develop a sense of what is most fitting for your situation.

Phases of Change

The columns of the matrix are defined by phases of change. Because many people have to think and act differently, it takes considerable time to fundamentally change a system. People and systems cannot be separated. As systems go through changes, so do the people involved in making the systems work. Although the process is complex and varies from school to school or community to community, there

Figure 11.2. Action and Inquiry Map for Cultivation Inquiry

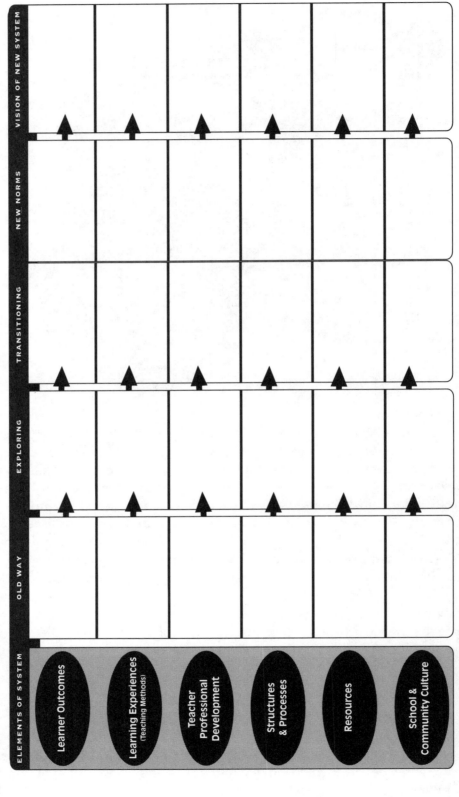

are, for purposes of description, four phases in the change process. These phases are, however, flexible and can flow together. They are congruent with other models of stages of change (Anderson [Parsons], 1993; Bridges, 1991; Land & Jarman, 1992; Parsons, 1998) and are described as follows:

- Maintenance of old ways
- Exploration of new outcomes and ways of operating
- Transition from the old to the new system
- New norms based on the vision of a new education system

The descriptions that follow are derived from research and from syntheses of evaluations of school change. They are intended not as the final word but as illustrations to help you think through your own situation. As you read through these descriptions and other research, consider how you would modify the phases to make them applicable to your school and what indicators you would use to determine your phase of change. Here is another "tight-light" situation. Hold tightly to the notion of making incremental progress but lightly to exact indicators, phases, and steps of the path.

Maintenance of Old Ways

In this stage, people expect to overcome problems and challenges by improving the approaches already in use rather than by trying a new approach. The power dynamics of dominant cultures and organizations are held firmly in place. Eventually, a few key people realize that if they continue to do what they have always done, they will continue to get the same (unsatisfactory) results, no matter how hard they try. Although a few small projects (probably led by people with little power) are attempting to change the system, it is unlikely that you will find initiatives aimed at changing the philosophical underpinnings of the school.

Exploration

The exploration stage often begins when key people realize that efforts to improve learning have made little or no difference in the life of students. They begin to wonder whether there might be a better approach. This can be a very frightening stage because people don't know what to do next. They feel guilty or unhappy about their performance, yet they fear letting go of the familiar. They begin to blame others. Getting past this frightened, blaming period is critical to the development of new initiatives and alternative practices. But often people will not begin to band together and let go of anger and blame until the Transition stage.

The Exploration stage is often characterized by tokenism on the part of people in power. They try to include those who have been excluded but they do so (whether consciously or unconsciously) in a way that ensures the locus of power remains the same. When collaboration or small projects are discussed, the conversations are embedded with distrust and a lack of commitment to new strategies. People are just beginning to break loose from their old paradigms and beginning to see other possibilities. As they hear of new ways of working and thinking and as tensions increase, they realize change is needed.

New ideas can come from many sources, but it is critical for educators to *see* the change in action and *hear* about it from their peers. Examples of sources are conferences, videotapes, study groups, Internet discussion groups, one-on-one conversations with stakeholders, and visits to schools experiencing success in an area of interest. Lots of turf issues and power struggles will occur as people try out new roles and responsibilities. But unless change starts to happen in all parts of the school (e.g. students, teachers, structures, and community relations), it is unlikely that the work will lead to significant change.

At the Exploration stage, people's understanding of the new practices and philosophies deepens, as does their ability to apply them. They come to recognize the connection between daily practice and underlying assumptions and beliefs as well as the incongruities between current practice and new beliefs and assumptions.

Watch out for several pitfalls during this stage. Examples of these are the adoption of a single technique to the exclusion of others or the feeble implementation of a strategy that dooms it to failure. Often, some stakeholders become such strong advocates for a chosen approach that they criticize others for not using it. This undermines the environment of trust and encouragement essential to move forward. At the opposite end are people so inundated with options that they try many at a very superficial level rather than at the depth needed to test their usefulness. Similarly, some may try new practices without challenging their fundamental beliefs about how systems need to operate or about how they view other people and the learning process.

The move from the Exploration to the Transition stage is typically the biggest leap from one stage to another—crossing a chasm. This is where you need a deep commitment to a new set of underlying principles about how systems should operate. Without this commitment, you will either get caught in an endless loop of explorations or will revert back to the old ways of doing business.

Transition

It is in the Transition stage that initiatives coalesce and new structures are put in place based on the new philosophy. Problems inevitably occur when you make the switch to the new system. Typically, people want to hang on to too many aspects of the old system until they are comfortable with the new ways. Those who succeed realize they don't have the resources to do both. This is a tricky process. Rather than throwing everything out from the past or trying to keep all of both old and new, you figure out what past practices also work in the new context and what new practices to develop. Then you decide how to allocate resources to support the change. Base these tough decisions on a deliberate commitment to the new underlying assumptions (e.g., a commitment to shared decision making rather than hierarchically based decisions).

During the Transition stage, resources are typically needed from outside sources; however, increasingly large amounts will be reallocated from within the existing formal and informal systems. For example, your school may decide that you will no longer pay for sports uniforms out of the school budget but instead spend those dollars on professional development and ask the community to raise funds to cover the cost of the uniforms.

The Transition stage is a fragile one. You will still need considerable outside support, both morally and financially. Yet all too often you will find that external supporters pull out after the Exploration stage, leaving initiatives too fragile to weather the assaults of those still holding onto their old power positions and perspectives. The Transition stage represents the dying of the old—letting go of past priorities and frameworks—and holding firm to the new vision.

New Norms

The stage referred to as New Norms is characterized by building the new in a habitual and committed fashion. Compare it to going beyond a periodic diet to a new set of long-term eating habits. At this point, those who may have been unwilling to commit before are finally convinced that this is the better way—or at least the one that is expected and will be rewarded. As you enter this stage, at least one third of the people in any stakeholder group are probably quite comfortable with the new way of doing things and regularly use new language and practices (e.g., shared decision making). Also, leaders within nearly all stakeholder groups are confident in their ability to build new norms from within and to leverage resources to further their goals.

When your school is firmly at this stage, key features that shape the school are operating in accord with the fundamental assumptions (results oriented, personalization) of the vision. Yet rather than saying that the vision is fully realized, I refer to this stage as New Norms because seldom, if ever, are new philosophies and practices fully in place. As your school approaches the desired way of being, you can expect to see something beyond that is even more desirable (see the "three C's" story in the book's introductory chapter).

Now, having learned a considerable amount about the process of change, your school is probably ready to recycle though the whole continuum again. Fortunately, key people have shifted to a learning mode and have created a "learning organization" or "learning community." By now, too, your school is more flexible, more able to incorporate small changes with less dramatic shifts in thinking and action than the first time your school worked through the process of fundamental redesign.

Because system change is a dynamic process, movement is constant—forward and backward—along and across the continuum. You will gradually develop a different perspective, recognizing patterns of change and gaining confidence in your preparation to face the inevitable next set of challenges. You are increasingly prepared to deal with the cycles of life.

Detailing the Cultivation AIM

After you have set up the Cultivation AIM matrix with the appropriate categories, you're ready to work with the Action Team to fill in the cells of the matrix. One approach is for the Action Team to divide into groups of two or three, each working on a row of the continuum. Those in each group might invite others to join them. Members of the working groups need to be knowledgeable about both their own school situation and the research on school change. The task is to develop indicators of what the school would look like at each stage. The more measurable the indicators

Figure 11.3. Winding Trail's Expanded Action and Inquiry Map

ELEMENTS OF SYSTEM	OLD WAY	EXPLORING	TRANSITIONING	NEW NORMS	VISION OF NEW SYSTEM
Learner Outcomes	• Learning based on seat time • Memorization and rote skills emphasized	• New student learning standards being discussed • Staff dialogue and study groups about standards and assessment of learning	• Emerging consensus on important student learning standards • Old concepts of learning replaced by focus on essential skills, knowledge, and lasting understandings • Student learning on desired outcomes showing noticeable improvement in a few key areas	Norm Is: • Desired long-term outcomes guide selection of short-term outcomes, curriculum materials, and assessment • Continual improvement in student learning for all students	• High standards for all students to learn meaningful skills, knowledge, and areas of lasting understanding • Focus on critical thinking and application of learning • Standards based on students' needs in a global society
Learning Experiences (Teaching Methods)	• Emphasis on textbook-based curriculum • Norm-referenced assessments methods • Teachers as deliverers of information • Students in passive receiver role • Disciplines kept separate	• Teachers explore new ways of teaching, visit other schools to observe new practices • Some teachers commit to piloting new teaching methods and evaluating impact on students	• At least 40% of teachers committed to new approaches and most of others open to possibilities • Recognition of depth of change needed • Teachers convinced change is not a fad • Changes in practice being evaluated	Norm Is: • Teaching methods actively engage and challenge students' thinking • Meaningful learning experiences • Connections across disciplines is the norm • Assessments encourage continual improvement	• Personalized instruction, a range of teaching strategies • Challenging student work, in-depth content • Learning extends beyond classroom • Students are active, engaged, responsible learners; teacher as coach
Teacher Professional Development	• Top-down decisions on content • Short-term, one-shot workshops with little or no follow up and coordination • Outside experts, "sit and get" format	• Recognition of need to connect professional development to student learning • Schoolwide staff needs assessment for professional development • Job-embedded professional development, peer assistance, mentoring initiated	• Professional development based on teacher and student needs is negotiated • School professional development committee with teacher leaders established • Community recognizing need for teacher professional development • Collegial, job-embedded professional development	Norm Is: • Professional development plans driven by student learning needs • Majority of teachers committed to collegial learning	• School-based learning communities with ongoing, job-embedded professional development for all teachers • Collegial, reflective, peer assistance and mentoring • Teacher designed and directed
Structures & Processes	• Hierarchical structure, top-down decision making • Policies designed largely as mandates	• Site-based decision making approaches piloted • Policies, structures, and processes reviewed	• Governance emphasizes shared responsibility and accountability • Policies revised to encourage collaboration, collegiality, standards-based learning • Alignment of policies around desired outcomes for students underway	Norm Is: • New processes to manage work congruent with high student standards, shared decision-making and accountability • Flexible structures the norm, including policy, administration and governance • Aligned policies	• Shared site-based decision making and leadership • Leaders support rather than control • Policies support collaborations, high standards of learning • Flexibility for achieving standards for diverse students
Resources	• Resource allocations based on inputs rather than outcomes • Little or no use of community as learning resource	• Budgets reviewed to determine how to align resources with desired outcomes • Community institutions contacted to determine resources for learning • New practices supported by grants or other special funds	• Policies changed to support resources allocated according to what is necessary to achieve learning outcomes for all students • Negotiate use of community resources for learning • New practices that work supported by regular funds	Norm Is: • Financial resources allocated to support vision • Human resources allocated to ensure high standards of learning for all students • Strong community-based learning for students and teachers	• School time and financial resources allocated by student learning goals (not by line item) • Community, administration, governance viewed as resource for learning
School & Community Culture	• Culture of control, following the rules • Community support of schools generally taken for granted • Public informed, not engaged, by schools	• Conscious attention to school norms • Conscious attention to community norms	• Articulate desired school norms • Articulate desired community norms regarding relationship to schools • Specific activities underway to adjust norms	Norm Is: • Parents and public are partners with the school and students in support of learning • Students hold positive view of active engagement in learning • Culture of collaboration, trust, respect	• Parents, students, educators, and community share responsibility for student learning • School and community cultures encourage high standards of learning for all students • Tone of decency, trust, respect

the better, as long as they still capture the essence of the stage. The indicators should reflect the desired philosophical shifts and the Cultivation to include more people. Once each group has worked out a progression for its row, the Action Team and Inquiry Team meet to compile the full matrix and make adjustments to create a meaningful whole.

Developing the AIM at Winding Trail High School

Winding Trail's School Renewal Committee, with assistance from the Inquiry Team, translated the principles into an AIM for its Sustainability inquiry three years ago. Last year, it developed an elaborated AIM using the stages of change described above. To work out a progression of change, the Inquiry Team began with the vision statement from its Sustainability AIM and worked backward through the stages, identifying indicators of each stage. Pairs from the School Renewal Committee each worked on one row of the matrix. One person from each pair then met to review the ideas from all the pairs. Building on these ideas, they refined the full matrix.

The Inquiry Team now uses the continuum on a regular basis. The Inquiry Team continues to track the Quality of learning in each department as well as the infrastructure changes and uses the continuum in the interpretation of the data. At the end of each year, the Inquiry Team facilitates a group process for those on the School Renewal Committee in which the members determine where they are on the continuum as part of the Vision-Action Synthesis.

After the Inquiry Team completes an inquiry cycle, it records changes in the vision based on the inquiry work. The School Renewal Committee keeps these records in a notebook with major documents about the school's change process. The committee plans to add the results of the ongoing Cultivation inquiry by beginning each year's section with the expanded AIM. Because seemingly glacial changes can get lost in everyday work, the School Renewal Committee expects that the progression of Cultivation AIMs will help it see the "deep currents" of change in the flow of Winding Trail High School. Those on the committee hope to find a rich evolution of change as they look back over the AIMs for several years. A copy of their current AIM is attached (see Figure 11.3).

In the meantime, the continuum serves as the basis for moving ahead on the Cultivation inquiry. Winding Trail High School was thus ready for the planning stage of the Cultivation inquiry for the second year of its use.

Planning the Cultivation Inquiry

Chapter Overview

The planning process for the Cultivation inquiry parallels that of the Quality and Sustainability inquiry designs. First, work with the users to refine the questions that are important to them related to the key issue, in this case, cultivation. Clarify how you will conduct your Vision-Action and Next Steps Syntheses based on these questions. Determine analyses that will address the questions guiding the syntheses. Determine what data to collect for the analyses, determine the budget, and confirm the Inquiry Team.

The differences between planning the Cultivation inquiry and the Quality and Sustainability inquiries rest with the questions that guide the work, which, in turn, result in different analyses and data collection. If the Cultivation inquiry is the appropriate design, the key questions will be something like these: How does the actual pattern of Cultivation compare to our envisioned patterns, and why? What are the implications for our next steps?

You use the same charts for developing tasks and timelines as you'd use for the Sustainability inquiry; issues of budget and Inquiry Team membership are essentially the same for both designs. I concentrate here on the syntheses, analyses, and data collection that are unique to the Cultivation inquiry design.

Guiding Syntheses and Analyses

In a Cultivation inquiry, the Vision-Action Synthesis answers this question: How does the actual pattern of cultivation compare to our envisioned pattern? It uses the Cultivation AIM discussed in Chapter 11.

The Next Steps Synthesis answers this two-part question: What accounts for the current position on the continuum, and what are the implications for our next steps? It draws on two analyses based on research findings. The first considers how innovations spread and the second how collaboration is built. I label these the Tipping Points analysis and the Collaboration analysis. Below is background information on the two analyses. Other more complex analyses could be added that are designed around specific features of the philosophical shifts.

Tipping Points Analysis

Types of Adopters

For many years, Everett Rogers has been compiling research across many fields on how innovations spread (see, e.g., Rogers, 1995). He has identified five types of people in terms of how readily they adopt innovations. A given person could be identified as one type in regard to one innovation and another type in regard to a second innovation.

Innovators. Innovators tend to be venturesome, eager to try new ideas, and not troubled by setbacks or the incompleteness of ideas or methods. They network quickly outside their local circles. (About 3% of the population)

Early Adopters. Early adopters are more a part of the local social system and contain local opinion leaders. They are not as far ahead of the average individual as innovators and are more trusted locally. (About 13%)

Early Majority. The early majority adopt new ideas just before the average person does. They seldom hold leadership positions. They tend to deliberate for quite some time before adopting an innovation and decide to adopt an innovation later than innovators and early adopters. (About 34%)

Late Majority. The late majority adopt new ideas just after the average person does. They often don't adopt something new until it is an economic necessity and/or there is growing peer pressure. They tend to have scarce resources and are therefore more reluctant to take risks. (About 34%)

Laggards. The laggards, the late minority, are the last to adopt an innovation or may never adopt it. They are not opinion leaders. They tend to be isolates and their point of reference is their past. (About 16%)

These categories probably seem familiar to you. Almost all whole school change starts with a group of enthusiastic teachers and administrators who have grasped that a school dominated by hierarchy and the delivery of information is fundamentally different from one designed around collaboration and the student-as-worker/teacher-as-coach concept. These educators are good at taking abstract ideas and translating them into practical changes in the school. They like to piece things together. They like to be in contact with national movements related to whole school change to see what others are doing, grab a few ideas, and build their own new courses and ways of operating. They can create pockets of change. But it is another matter to move beyond them to get the bulk of teachers, students, and community members operating in a new way.

The challenge: How do you move from the innovators and early adopters to the early and late majority? Some researchers and writers talk about a "chasm" between those who adopt an innovation early and the majority (Moore, 1991). Others talk about a "tipping point" (Gladwell, 2000). Once the chasm is crossed or tipping point reached, adoption of the innovation (in this case, new principles to guide school operations) is accelerated.

Creators of Tipping Points

Research on tipping points (Gladwell, 2000) leads to several ideas that may help a school identify ways to accelerate whole school change. I built an analysis that helps develop understanding of the whole school change initiative from four features of Gladwell's work: (a) key influencers, (b) stickiness, (c) subtle signals, and (d) small groups. (I use slightly different terminology than Gladwell uses.)

Key Influencers. Some people matter more than others do in most processes and systems. Innovations are driven by a handful of exceptional people—connoisseurs, connectors, and marketers. The behaviors that make a difference are how sociable, energetic, knowledgeable, or influential among peers they are. Connoisseurs are data banks. They accumulate knowledge and like to share information with others to help them improve their lives. They provide the content. Connectors are social glue; they spread the message, product, or ideas. Connectors are linked to everyone else in just a few steps. They have a special gift for bringing people together. Marketers have the skill to bring in the unconvinced.

Stickiness. An important part of communication is ensuring that a message makes an impact on its target audience. "Stickiness" describes how much is remembered. To spark the spread of an innovation, ideas have to be memorable and move people to action. Once information or advice becomes practical and personal, it becomes memorable. Gladwell says there are some small, subtle, and easy ways to make a message "stick," which in turn can create a tipping point within a particular situation.

Subtle Signals. Human behavior is a lot more suggestible than it seems. People are very sensitive to environmental cues and changes in context. So, small and subtle factors can serve as tipping points in the spreading of innovations. Gladwell explains the power of context with the "broken window theory," which says that a small condition such as a broken window may convey a signal that no one cares about a neighborhood, leading others to commit more serious crimes there.

Small Groups. Small, close-knit groups have the power to magnify the epidemic potential of a message or idea. Gladwell refers to "The Rule of 150," which says that the maximum number of individuals with whom a person can have a genuine social relationship is 150. Thus, for groups to be effective in operations based on personal relationships, the group should contain fewer than 150 members. And because innovations don't move effortlessly from one group to the next, connectors, connoisseurs, and marketers assume essential roles when they take ideas from one specialized group and translate them into language that other groups can understand. Once the ideas are in the new group, the closeness of that group helps spread the idea.

Collaboration Analysis

Closely related to the Rule of 150 is the importance of collaboration. In collaborative environments, information flows with relative ease. Genuine collaboration, which develops over time, promotes thoughtful interaction about what is being shared. In a study of collaborations among districts, schools, teachers' associations, universities, and communities to encourage high-quality professional development for teachers (Parsons & Lupe, 2000), Carolyn Lupe and I distinguished three levels of collaboration, which are discussed below. They serve as the basis for the collaboration analysis.

Low Collaboration

Sites experiencing low collaboration tend to use these words to characterize their situation—*hierarchy, distrust, conflict,* and *adversarial relationships.* In some cases, it seems that the relationships are set up because people know they should work together but have not learned the skills needed for collaborative work, do not want to collaborate, and/or don't have structures in place to guide the collaboration. Some partners sign on but then don't participate.

Transition to Collaboration

When sites transition from adversarial and hierarchical relationships to collaborative ones, participants describe their situation as one where people *listen and learn.* They begin to *develop trust and respect.* They undertake *common tasks* that benefit all of them. During this phase, *certain organizational policies and practices* begin to form that provide a means by which people can come together and learn from one another (e.g., cross-role committees).

High Collaboration

The following characterize groups (and individuals) that collaborate well:

◆ Trust and respect

- Open communication (listen and learn)
- Creative thinking
- Shared leadership around priority issues
- Mutually beneficial work and contributions
- Policies, practices, and structures created to intentionally bring people together
- Celebration of accomplishments
- Renewal and cultivation

One-to-one relationships build trust and successful collaboration on the larger scale. In fully collaborative relationships, *trust,* grounded in mutual *respect,* has been firmly established. Even though people may still disagree, they do so with an attitude of respect for one another's opinions and person. They become able and willing to express their genuine feelings, beliefs, and values and to listen to those of others. As they develop skills of effective dialogue (Senge et al., 1994), the *open communication* leads to *creative thinking* because the voices of many different people with multiple perspectives produce richer discussions and more creative solutions. Increased buy-in and more authentic and sustainable action result. Strong, committed individuals within and across the collaborating groups drive collaboration. Over time, more people take on *leadership* roles, sharing the workload and expanding the forces moving in a common direction. All parties *contribute* and *benefit* in appropriate and important ways.

At the full collaboration stage, the *collaborative structures* and agreements have been formalized into *policies.* These policies, in turn, help frame, guide, and sustain the collaboration. For example, district and teachers' association policies that support jointly sponsored professional development help keep work on track even when there are changes in leadership.

The collaboration is nurtured and maintained over time by *celebrating accomplishments, renewing* bonds, revisiting the shared vision and making adjustments, and *expanding* collaborations to include other organizations and the community (for information on additional factors influencing the success of collaboration, see Mattessich & Monsey, 1992).

Collecting Data for the Analyses

To do a Tipping Points analysis, you need data about the mix of connoisseurs, connectors, and marketers; the stickiness of the message; the nature of small signals in the daily context of the school; and the cohesiveness within and across small groups. For the Collaboration analysis, you need data about the extent and nature of collaboration among key groups. A variety of data collection techniques—interviews, focus groups, observations, and questionnaires, to name a few—can be used to gather this information. Here is how Winding Trail High School approached data collection.

Planning Data Collection at Winding Trail High School

Last spring, Winding Trail worded its Challenge Statement as "insufficient progress in improved learning for all students." When the school's Inquiry Team conducted its annual Vision-Action Synthesis based on the expanded AIM the previous fall, the team concluded that students were not engaged in learning. It wanted to understand why and planned to use the Tipping Points and Collaboration analyses as the basis for that understanding; it would shape the Next Steps Synthesis.

Before determining how to approach data collection, one Inquiry Team member wrote a short synopsis of the Tipping Points book. At a study session during one of the team's meetings, the members discussed it.

Small Groups

The Inquiry Team identified a variety of student groups in the school. They were defined by participation in sports; by neighborhood and ethnicity; by academic achievement; by preferences for subject areas; by social popularity; and by interest in computers. Certain core classes such as language arts, history, and math tended to be grouped by grade level. The Inquiry Team identified about eight groups that contained most of the students in addition to their participation by grade level.

Key Influencers

As a means of discovering key influencers among students, the Inquiry Team decided to first identify the teachers whom it thought were most knowledgeable about students in each of these small groups and then asked these teachers to identify students who fit the following descriptions:

1. Who tends to accumulate knowledge and likes to share information with others to help them improve their lives?
2. Who serves as the "social glue," spreading messages, products, or ideas?
3. Who can persuade others about something when they are unconvinced?

This kind of informal method of identifying key influences can achieve satisfactory results, although more sophisticated methods that involve developing sociograms are also available (Schensul, 1999; Schensul & LeCompte, 1999).

Stickiness

To determine the stickiness of the message about engaging in learning, the Inquiry Team decided to enlist the aid of those teachers who seemed to have the most connections to influential students in each group. The Inquiry Team wanted the teachers to find out how these students would answer the following questions:

1. What makes learning about [fill in appropriate content area] attractive to you and your friends?

2. What makes learning about [fill in appropriate content area] unattractive to you and your friends?

Teachers were given latitude to ask these questions using the methods they deemed most appropriate. Acceptable approaches included written questions, informal questions to individual students, and class projects where students interviewed each other.

Subtle Signals

The Inquiry Team planned to conduct observations themselves as well as through student connoisseurs (knowledge accumulators). Students could receive credit for participating in hour-long observations. The planned method for these observations involved students simply walking around the school, reading what was on bulletin boards, and watching and listening to students in the hall. In this way, the Inquiry Team hoped to pick up and report back the subtle signals in the environment that encouraged or discouraged learning toward high standards.

Collaboration

For the Collaboration analysis, the Inquiry Team developed a rubric from the description of levels of collaboration given above. It also convened a group of students to determine what collaboration looked like within classrooms.

Tasks and Time Frame

Since an accreditation visit was scheduled for February and the Inquiry Team wanted to include the results as part of its self-study report, the team needed to be on a fast track. So it set November 30th as the completion date for its data collection, analysis and synthesis.

When the School Renewal Committee members received the data collection and analysis planning charts from the Inquiry Team, they were intrigued by the approach. They helped refine the wording of the data collection questions and worked out ways to approach teachers and students so as to avoid any problematic labeling of students in their identification of "key influencers."

Cultivation Inquiry Data Collection, Analysis, Synthesis, and Communication of Results

Chapter Overview

This chapter uses the Winding Trail High School example to illustrate one approach to data collection, analysis, synthesis, and communications of results in a

Cultivation inquiry. A variety of data collection methods could be used to gather data that would then feed into the Tipping Points and Collaboration analyses. These analyses along with the data from the ongoing Quality and Sustainability inquiries provide the basis for the Vision-Action and Next Steps syntheses.

Data Collection at Winding Trail High School

Tipping Points Analysis

Small Groups and Key Influencers

Jim, one member of the Inquiry Team, prepared an informal survey form for selected teachers to use to identify key influencers within various groups. The form, which could be filled out in five or ten minutes, also contained Jim's e-mail address so that teachers could send him e-mail messages with additional names. He summarized the forms and tallied the number of times each student was mentioned in each category.

Inquiry Team members selected one of the identified groups and asked three or four teachers to fill out the form for the group he/she was investigating. Before giving the form to a teacher to complete, the Inquiry Team member wrote a description of the group at the top of the form.

Subtle Signals

Kelly, another Inquiry Team member, was responsible for taking the lead on the Subtle Signals data collection. She developed a "report form" for the school observers using a stack of colored 3-by-5-inch cards, convened small groups of data collectors to explain what they should look for, and gave each data collector a code number and placed this number on the cards given to the person. She set up drop boxes in the library, cafeteria, main office, and department offices so people could write down ideas as they thought of them. She asked the data collectors to put one description on each card and drop it in one of the boxes. For those who preferred to communicate electronically, Kelly provided her e-mail address.

As an incentive, she offered free movie tickets (donated by a local theater) to those contributing the top five ideas. The cards made it easy for her to sort ideas and quickly identify patterns. They were looking for subtle signals—the palm-to-the-forehead ("Why didn't I think of that?") kind—so the "top" ideas weren't necessarily the ones receiving the most votes.

Stickiness

Another Inquiry Team member, Roy, organized focus groups to discuss the guiding question "What will make learning more meaningful and interesting for students?" He selected the students and teachers for the focus groups after the key influencers data had been collected and also selected a mix of connoisseurs, connectors, and marketers. He asked each member of these groups to identify two community members who tended to gather and share ideas with others. From those identified, Roy organized two community groups composed of individuals who cut across the social and economic groups of the community. Neighborhood association leaders proved eager to help arrange the focus sessions, for the sessions brought people into the centers and expanded their connections to the community and school. After the various groups discussed the guiding question, they talked about individual subject areas (e.g., health, math, social studies, science, sports, fine arts, and language arts) as well as other subjects they identified as important.

Collaboration

The Inquiry Team developed a rubric of low, medium, and high collaboration using the characteristics discussed during its planning step. The team identified the groups whose collaboration seemed critical to the success of whole school change and asked School Renewal Committee members to rate the level of collaboration among these groups and the rationale for their rating:

♦ Students–teachers
♦ Teachers–administrators
♦ Teachers' association–district leaders
♦ School board members–administrators
♦ Parents–school leaders
♦ Groups within the student body
♦ Cross-department collaboration

The Inquiry Team averaged the ratings for each pairing and drew a diagram depicting the level of collaboration among the various parties. To test the accuracy of these results, the team used its key influencers list to select a few people in each category who would review and comment on the diagram. The Inquiry Team also held a few small focus groups composed of students identified as key influencers. These student groups talked about what it meant to have good collaboration within the classroom and school and the extent to which it existed.

Analyzing the Data at Winding Trail High School

Tipping Points

Two of the Inquiry Team members consolidated the information about the small groups and the key influencers within and among the groups. They grouped them as connoisseurs, connectors, and marketers and used this information to determine whom to include in the focus groups. The Inquiry Team would use this information again later in its communication plan. From the stickiness data, it found that many students did not find the current student learning to be sufficiently meaningful to be "sticky." It did not have sufficient connection to the real world either locally or globally. Technology was not adequately used, and the school did not connect to community residents and businesses. The school needed to change from trying to get the community involved in the school to getting the school involved in the community.

Community members' opinions revealed similar themes. Community members and students were not adequately involved in shaping the way the school operated and what it was attempting to accomplish for students.

The Subtle Signals analysis showed that students did not think that many teachers were genuinely interested in either their content area or the students in a personal way. A large number of teachers seemed more interested in getting out of school as quickly as possible. They did not take personal time to deepen their knowledge of their discipline. Teachers did not talk to students in the halls except to reprimand them. Students were not very respectful to one another, and teachers did not consistently model respectful behavior either.

Collaboration

The Inquiry Team found good collaboration between the school board, on the one hand, and the school and district administration, on the other. The relationship between the teachers' association and the school board is becoming less adversarial. Other findings on collaboration across the board included frequent examples of lack of conscious recognition of the importance of collaboration, lack of insight into how to achieve a healthy blend of hierarchy and collaboration at all levels of the system and with the community, and little collaboration between the school and community businesses or residents.

Synthesizing Findings

Steps in a Vision-Action Synthesis

Information from the Tipping Points and Collaboration analyses along with ongoing Quality and Sustainability inquiry analyses builds a strong knowledge base for the Vision-Action Synthesis. As many as 50 people can be involved in the process, which can be used with school faculty, administrators, students, and/or community members. If several different groups are engaged in the synthesis, you can compare the results from the different groups. Members of the Inquiry Team or an outside person would serve as the facilitator of the process and recorder of the synthesis and key points of the discussions.

There are nine steps in the synthesis process:

1. Provide a summary of the information from the Tipping Points and Collaboration analyses along with results from available Quality and Sustainability inquiry analyses to those involved in the synthesis. The information can be provided in writing or through oral presentations. A combination of methods works well, as does giving group members time

to discuss the results. The common set of data helps people see a bigger picture as they develop their interpretation of the situation.

2. On the meeting room wall, post a very large (4-by-6-foot) reproduction of the AIM in Figure 11.2. The rows and columns of the AIM are labeled, and all the cells are left blank.

3. Give everyone a copy of the AIM with all information in all cells of the matrix (such as Figure 11.3). Discuss the right-hand column, explaining that it describes the desired vision for the school as defined by the whole school change initiative. Give the group an opportunity to review the AIM and determine whether the components of the AIM represent the intended philosophy or expected pattern of change. Unless there are major issues that need to be discussed, have the participants note changes on their own copy of the AIM before analyzing the status of the initiative. The changes will be collected later.

4. Divide the large group into small groups of two to six people. You may choose to have cross-role groups or role-alike groups depending on which configuration you think will create the most insightful discussions.

5. Using a copy of the AIM at their table, the members of each group put sticky notes on the cell in each row that that they think corresponds to the current phase of change at the school. On these sticky notes they identify the data that support their group's thinking. Ask the groups to consider the school as a whole drawing heavily on their own firsthand experience and knowledge (e.g., teachers' knowledge of their own departments) along with the summary of results of the Inquiry Team's work. Each group transfers its sticky notes to the large version of the AIM on the wall. Sometimes, people will not want to select one cell in a row. If so, they can divide the sticky note across several phases. Remember that your priority is to generate genuine insights into the situation rather than to determine a fixed position.

6. Discuss the patterns that emerge and the extent of agreement. For example, you are likely to find that some parts of the system are farther along in the phases of change than others. It is important to communicate that there is no one right pattern of moving forward. In some situations, teachers' learning (professional development) may lead, and in other cases, the teaching and learning practices or school-community climate/culture may be farther ahead. The key part of the analysis is to determine if some components are lagging behind or are too far ahead. Ultimately, you want all parts of the system to be roughly on the right-hand side. If the spread among the components gets too great along the way, considerable tension is likely and the change process may collapse or be significantly stalled.

7. Notes taken by the Inquiry Team recorder should capture key points of discussion that may not be evident from the placement of sticky notes on the continuum. It is also helpful to have the recorder list who was present so the team can describe the type of people who participated in the process.

8. After the AIM analysis is complete, ask those participating to review the right-hand column of the AIM (the "vision" column). Ask them to write

on the AIM or on a separate sheet of paper any changes they think should be made in the vision.

9. The Inquiry Team uses recorded comments, sticky notes, and changes written on the individual copies of the AIM to compile a summary of the analysis. Ultimately, the School Renewal Committee uses this information to revisit the vision and make needed adjustments in the vision or phases of change.

Winding Trail Syntheses

Vision-Action Synthesis

Using the information from the Quality and Sustainability work as well as the information from the Tipping Points and Collaboration analyses, the Inquiry Team used the above process to determine where the school as a whole is on the expanded AIM. In other words, how close is Winding Trail to achieving its vision?

The conclusion was that the school was at the following points on the AIM:

Student Learning Outcomes	Exploring/Transitioning
Teaching and Learning Experiences for Students	Transitioning
Teacher Learning (Professional Development)	Exploring/Transitioning
Structures and Processes	Exploring/Transitioning
Resources	Exploring
School-Community Culture	Exploring

Next Steps Synthesis

Using the Vision-Action Synthesis and the analyses that supported it, the Inquiry Team developed a set of considerations for the School Renewal Committee. The team concluded that it was going to be necessary to involve students and the community to a far greater extent to make learning meaningful to students. The Inquiry Team suggested that the School Renewal Committee sponsor a low-key, informal series of meetings among the student, faculty, and community members identified as key influencers. At these meetings, the groups would review the student learning standards and learning experiences to see what changes were needed. Once they had identified a core set of changes, they would meet with those responsible for teachers' professional development to identify well-targeted professional development experiences to build faculty capacity in addressing these learning outcomes and in using teaching methods that would actively engage students. With concrete plans of the needed professional development, they would meet with administrators and policymakers to determine how to make strategic changes in structures, processes, and resources to highlight these outcomes and teaching methods and to provide teachers with the necessary professional development. The fact that the school board and teachers' association leaders are seeking a collaborative relationship was considered an important opportunity.

The Inquiry Team felt that Winding Trail should institute a yearly assessment of the climate of the school and of the relationship between the school and the community. It recommended setting up a subcommittee of the School Renewal Committee to work with the Inquiry Team to develop this assessment device, building on the assessment instrument they were already using to assess the climate from the perspective of teachers and administrators. See www.InSites.org for an example of a climate instrument adopted from the Readiness for Organizational Learning and Evaluation Instrument (ROLE) (Preskill & Torres, 2000).

Communicating Inquiry Results

Points to Consider

The users of a Vision-Action Synthesis for a Cultivation inquiry design need to interact with the analyses and the expanded AIM to understand the findings. Simply presenting the results of the Inquiry Team's Vision-Action and Next Steps Syntheses to the primary user is typically not very effective. A more effective approach is to have the users work through the Vision-Action Synthesis themselves. Then the Inquiry Team can share its synthesis and discuss similarities and differences. At this point, the Inquiry Team can present its Next Steps Synthesis as a starting point for further development with the Action Team.

It's useful to keep the communications very interactive and help the users see the broad picture, including both the full range of features that need to be considered and the details about key characteristics found through the Tipping Points and Collaboration analyses. By working through the Vision-Action Synthesis, they engage in rich discussion about the status of the initiative. Contrasting their synthesis with that of the Inquiry Team serves as a reliability check and generates another level of discussion.

Building a trusting, respectful, learning community is the foundation of the communication strategy. Usually, when working with the users beyond the Action Team you need only describe the results of the Vision-Action Synthesis and then concentrate on the results of the Next Steps Synthesis. Provide concrete changes for the external and internal partners to work on, that is, changes clearly focused on student learning as well as professional development well embedded in their everyday work, not add-ons. Also, use methods that build high-quality collaborative relationships throughout the school and community. Build a strong sense that the education of students is the responsibility of the whole community.

Winding Trail Communications

The Inquiry Team met with the School Renewal Committee in a half-day session, where it engaged the committee in the same process the team had used to conduct the Vision-Action Synthesis. After the School Renewal Committee had completed its synthesis, the Inquiry Team shared its synthesis. The results were very similar. Next, the committee reviewed the Inquiry Team's ideas about the Next Steps Synthesis. It developed a strategy to build an informal network of communications among the key influencers in each of the groups and would use this network to explore ways to communicate results and to engage the influencers' participation.

The School Renewal Committee decided to wait until after the accreditation team's visit to formally communicate the results of the inquiry work. Before suggesting their next steps, those on the committee wanted to get the reactions of the accreditation team and to learn more from the key influencers within the various groups.

Conclusion: Enriching and Continuing the Evaluative Inquiry Process

Chapter Overview

You now have a five-step process to inquire into three features of programs and initiatives that are at the heart of successful change—quality, sustainability, and cultivation. The process encourages you to look beyond whether people like a program or activity and focus on the fundamental features that shape an initiative's likelihood of improving student learning over the long haul. The evaluative inquiry method is designed to help gradually redesign fundamental features of your school.

I have described the inquiry process and designs in a very basic form. As you gain more and more skill, you can use them in increasingly complex situations and add analyses. These inquiry designs and the five steps of inquiry are core processes for continual improvement. But they are just that—core processes, not the finished picture of ongoing implementation of evaluative inquiry. Just as the program continually improves, so too the inquiry process can be continually improved. I recently heard someone say that if you improved by 1/1000 every day, you would improve by 26% over the course of a year. (I didn't check his math.) Small incremental strategic changes lead to substantial improvement over time. The evaluative inquiry process is part of a new infrastructure to support continual learning and the transformation of the fundamental beliefs and assumptions on which the education system rests. It enables you to keep pace with the complexities of today's world.

Now that you are familiar with the three designs and the process for carrying them out, let's take a moment to reflect on three practices that will help you apply the designs successfully:

1. Keeping evaluative inquiry focused on continual improvement and student learning

2. Incorporating new research findings into evaluative inquiry

3. Enriching your evaluative inquiry capabilities

Improving Student-Focused Learning

My primary reason for presenting these evaluative inquiry designs is to increase your capacity to take charge of the changes going on in your school. They are intended to support you in being proactive in your communications about what changes are being made, how the changes are working, and what you are learning from your work. The designs can help move educators from a defensive posture to one of taking charge of their work and learning. Evaluative inquiry combines attention to the core relationship of teaching and learning, with a focus on improvement rather than proof to outsiders.

Often, evaluation and accountability create an environment where educators are afraid to look closely and systematically at the relationship between the changes they are making and student learning because the findings will be used to criticize rather than to encourage. So they look at superficial matters that give them a better chance of looking good to outsiders. These designs encourage you to gather the best data you can, then interact with one another around what you discover from the data to achieve a strong position focused on your vision.

As you develop the combined tools of using data along with well-designed formats for dialogue, you can generate major insights. Don't shy away from looking at the core relationship of teaching and learning; consider it in the context of the infrastructure. Develop a methodology of investigation that combines the best data you can gather about teaching and learning with effective methods of analysis, dialogue, collaboration, and trust among those who take responsibility for student learning.

These methods create a learning community. Welcome those willing to share responsibility. Extend, rather than defend, the boundaries of shared responsibility by including critics who are willing to share responsibility for improving learning.

Incorporating New Research Findings

Because so much new knowledge is being generated so quickly, the designs discussed here intentionally encourage you to keep bringing in new research findings. In particular, bring in new knowledge to the development of the vision as expressed in the Action and Inquiry Map and in the analysis methods. Recall that the designs encourage evolution of the vision as well as evolution of the way the program is implemented. When the Inquiry Team, Action Team, and others interact around the Vision-Action Synthesis, it is an excellent time to discuss any new knowledge that was unavailable when the vision was constructed. The Action Team may want to adjust its vision in areas ranging from the infrastructure to teaching and learning to processes of change.

A second way to incorporate new knowledge is to create new analytic tools based on research findings For example, in cases where a key part of the infrastructure of an initiative is a school-university partnership, I add analytic tools built from research on successful partnerships. The features can be converted into a rubric for use as an analytic tool during a Sustainability inquiry. They also can be used to enhance a Cultivation inquiry.

Sometimes, people are afraid to build in new research findings because they are afraid of being held accountable in areas not previously deemed important. Unfortunately, they slip into the mind-set of the outside judge rather than seeing the rubric as a way to help clarify the journey toward the desired future. This legitimate fear reinforces the importance of keeping the inquiry in the hands of the school faculty, who can ensure that the findings are used to improve, not to prove or blame.

Enriching Evaluative Inquiry Capacities

You can apply the designs and processes presented in this book in increasingly complex situations as you gain more and more inquiry capacities. Here are five areas that I focus on to develop my capacities:

- ◆ Team and community building
- ◆ Developing student learning outcomes and measures
- ◆ Evaluation and research methods
- ◆ Systems thinking and systems change
- ◆ Content knowledge

What follows are a few ideas and useful references for your evaluative inquiry library.

Team and Community Building

The evaluative inquiry designs rest on the premise that insight is gained through creative reflection on qualitative and quantitative data in a trusting, respectful, supportive environment. One fundamental technique embedded in these designs is honest communication. It enables groups to create something beyond what any one of them would generate alone.

Groups that have achieved this dynamic exhibit mutual respect; they listen to one another; they can express their point of view honestly without hostility or defensiveness. People are given the time, space, and encouragement to articulate their values and understand how they are expressed or undermined through particular actions. As Michael Fullan (1993) says, "Alliances are the bread and butter of learning organizations in dynamically complex societies" (p. 93).

Find books, seminars, and other resources that help you learn and practice these skills. Many resources exist, such as books by Peter Senge and his colleagues, in particular, *The Fifth Discipline Fieldbook* (Senge, Kleiner, Roberts, Ross, & Smith, 1994) and *Schools That Learn* (Senge et al., 2000). Other books include *The Wisdom of Teams* (Katzenbach & Smith, 1993), and *The TeamNet Factor* (Lipnach & Stamps, 1993). Books that help incorporate the community perspective include *The Careless Society* (McKnight, 1995) and *Building Communities From the Inside Out* (McKnight & Kretzmann, 1993). Good articles and books are also available about building learning communities, collaboration, and alliances (e.g., Fullan, 1993; Mattessich & Monsey, 1992; Parsons, 1998, 1999; Torres, Preskill, & Piontek, 1996).

Student Learning Outcomes and Measures

Creating learning outcomes that address deep understanding and knowing how to assess that understanding are important skills for evaluative inquiry. For information on ways to use performance assessments in schools and general knowledge about assessment of student and teacher learning, see Wiggins and McTighe (1998) and Stiggins (1994, 2000) as well as their respective Web sites (www.relearning.org and assessmentinst.org). Also check out the Web sites and publications of the professional associations in various disciplines such as the National Council of Teachers of Mathematics or the National Council of Teachers of English. Social services groups also have excellent resources on creating outcomes (e.g., The Learning Institute for Nonprofit Organizations, 2000; Reisman & Clegg, 2000; United Way of America, 1996).

Evaluation, Inquiry, and Research Methods

Evaluation Standards

The field of evaluation has established standards of practice that will benefit your evaluative inquiry. Jim Sanders (2000) provides an appendix with the widely recognized standards for program evaluation established by the Joint Committee on Standards for Education Evaluation. You can go to the Web site of the American Evaluation Association (www.eval.org) and obtain its set of guiding principles for conducting evaluations.

Evaluation and Research Perspectives

Many fine books exist about evaluation in general. Joellen Killion (2001) and Thomas Guskey (2000) have excellent books about evaluation of professional development. Jim Sanders (2000) wrote a basic evaluation book for educators, and Worthen et al. (1997) prepared a thorough book on the broad field of evaluation. Michael Patton (1997) wrote a very readable book on the utilization of evaluation, and Dan Stufflebeam (2001) produced a monograph that discusses 22 evaluation models.

By reading about both evaluation and research designs, you can distinguish between designs appropriate for your situation and those better applied to larger scale research. A classic book on research designs is by Campbell and Stanley (1966). Gall, Borg, and Gall (1996) provide a thorough introduction to research. After several years of a program's implementation, you may want more rigorous inquiry designs to compare and contrast variations of a program. If all the school's faculty are thinking along these lines, they can progressively structure their piloting of new techniques and content for more rigorous investigations.

Ethnographic research methods can be useful. Check out Evelyn Jacob's (1999) book about evaluating cooperative learning with qualitative methods or the *Ethnographer's Toolkit* (Schensul & LeCompte, 1999) or a method for studying your own school using qualitative methods (Anderson, Herr, & Nihlen, 1994).

Specific Data Collection and Analysis Techniques

Numerous books exist on developing and using particular data collection instruments (e.g., Bernard, 2000). You can find books on conducting focus groups (Krueger & Casey, 2000); doing surveys and writing questionnaires (Cox, 1996; Fowler, 1995; Thomas, 1999); doing classroom observations (Simon & Boyer, 1974); developing checklists (www.wmich.edu/evalctr); and interviewing (Gordon, 1980), to name a few. Other books will help you develop ways to track student performance and relate it to programmatic changes (Bernhardt, 1998; Herman & Winters, 1992). Many books provide basic statistical techniques (e.g., Bracey, 1997; Gall et al., 1996).

Systems Thinking and Systems Change

The designs addressing sustainability and cultivation are greatly enhanced by deepening your understanding of systems thinking and systems change. Again, Peter Senge's work in this field is very valuable. You can incorporate his system dynamics diagrams in the designs in this book to understand sustainability and cultivation (see Senge, 1990; Senge et al., 1994, 1999).

A leading writer and thinker about systems change in education is Michael Fullan, whose books (Fullan, 1993, 1999, 2001) give ideas that can help you design evaluative inquiries that produce new insights into your work. I also find it useful to read books on change and organizational structure from the business world (e.g., Bridges, 1991; Land & Jarman, 1992; Mintzberg, 1979; Moore, 1991; Price, Waterhouse Change Integration Team, 1995; Wheatley, 2001).

Closely tied to systems thinking is understanding the philosophy or mental models that shape a system. Senge talks extensively about mental models. Embedded in many of the changes occurring in education today are shifts in mental models regarding teaching and learning (Banathy, 1991; Bransford, Brown, &

Cocking, 1999) as well as mental models related to professionalism, bureaucracy, and community building (Parsons, 1998). These shifts are especially important to understand when using the Cultivation inquiry design.

Content Knowledge

Content knowledge may be disciplinary content, such as geography, or knowledge of pedagogy, management, or leadership that supports student learning. Although many evaluative inquiry skills are generic and can be applied across content areas, knowledge of the content being investigated strengthens your analytic abilities.

Closing Comments

My goal in writing this book has been to share with you some of what I have learned over the years that may help you continually improve the link between your work and results for students. Hopefully, the ideas will strengthen your focus on a high vision for student learning as well as your own learning; give those of you who are teachers greater control over the way your school operates; help you as administrators and policymakers create the conditions, encourage the practices, and enact the policies that support teachers' continual learning from their daily practice; provide you who are school coaches with additional tools; and support the transformation of schools into learning communities that are ever extending their embrace of those who want to learn and work together.

At the beginning of this book I talked about the climate of constant change that is enveloping educators today. In this climate, educators are coping with changes occurring around them and bringing needed changes into the education system. The inevitable question is this: Do your changes matter? Have you made changes that will bring more effective learning to students and to teachers? Through evaluative inquiry you can find out which changes matter for you.

Afterword: Change Matters

Most attempts at school reform have failed. Even those that have succeeded have been short lived and/or have failed to go to scale (Fullan, 2001a). In our own work, and in examining similar research, we have coined the 3-6-8 rule, meaning that it takes about 3 years to turn around an elementary school from poor performance to good performance as measured by student progress, about 6 years to turn around a high school, and about 8 years for a whole district.

There are three problems with these findings, as valid as they are. First, in the face of complex, urgent problems, many people feel that the timeline is too long. They ask whether these timelines can be accelerated—say, reduced by half. Second, only a small proportion of schools or districts that should be improving are actually doing so. This is the problem of scale. Third, and most revealing, it takes a great deal of effort to accomplish the turnaround, which can be undone almost overnight if two or three key people leave. Thus, sustaining reform remains elusive.

One of the prime reasons why reform cannot be accomplished is that people, especially groups of people, lack the capacity to engage in continuous reform processes. This is where Beverly Parsons's *Evaluative Inquiry* comes into play. As Parsons notes, there is a great deal of "information" available. Databases without a means of acting on them amount to information glut. As I, and others, have observed, information only becomes knowledge when it is socially processed (Brown & Duguid, 2000; Fullan, 2001b). In other words, people (teachers and principals, for example) must work together to move from information to action. For that they need to conceptualize how to go about it, and they need a set of skills and processes that will enable them to move forward.

Parsons's evaluative inquiry framework is a gold mine of ideas and designs. She bases the framework on three design components that effectively address the flaws in the 3-6-8 rule. One design element addresses Quality—does the initiative promote high-quality learning? The second focuses on Sustainability—can the initiative be sustained? And the third takes up the issue of going to scale, or Cultivation—can the initiative be cultivated beyond a small endeavor?

There are a number of significant features of Parsons's Action and Inquiry Map. First, it is based on vision as an evolving force. Second, it focuses on both student learning and teacher learning, demonstrating their close reciprocal relationship. Third, it distinguishes between short-term learning outcomes and long-term teacher learning outcomes. Fourth, and unlike most inquiry models in the literature, the model maps out system infrastructure in three main sections: Structure/Processes, Resources, and Culture. Structure/Processes contains several key elements (e.g., district/school leadership, assessment, and professional development); Resources includes district funds as well as human resources; and Culture incorporates norms about diversity, learning about many cultures, and so on. A rating form is provided in which readers can rate their own district on the 19 dimensions of structure, resources and culture. Parsons then outlines a process and set of steps for analyzing, supporting, and inhibiting factors in relation to the 19 dimensions. This enables her to map out four key patterns, distinguishing among no change versus disruptive change versus sporadic change versus continuous change.

At a time when most school systems suffer from overload, fragmentation, and multiple innovations colliding, Parsons provides a framework that is at once complex, accessible, and comprehensive. This book puts the process in the hands of teachers, principals, students, and community members. It takes into account the big picture of state-level policies and concerns.

In this time of fragmentation, Parsons shows how inquiry can move from analysis toward synthesis and communication; and how this evaluative process can be deepened and built in as a continuous process.

Evaluative Inquiry contains plenty of case examples, demonstrating how the evaluative inquiry process works in real situations. Capacity to manage complexity is the resource needed in the 21st century. Parsons has helped set us on an irreversible path. Once groups of people practice what she advocates, once they seek the products of evaluative inquiry and the tangible student and teacher results, it will be impossible to turn back.

—Michael Fullan
Dean, Ontario Institute for Studies in Education
University of Toronto

References for Afterword

Brown, J. S., & Duguid, P. (2000). *The social life of information.* Boston: Harvard Business School Press.

Fullan, M. (2001a). *The new meaning of educational change* (3rd ed.). New York: Teachers College Press.

Fullan, M. (2001b). *Leading in a culture of change.* San Francisco: Jossey-Bass.

References

Anderson [Parsons], B. L. (1993). The stages of systemic change. *Educational Leadership, 51*(1), 14-17.

Anderson, G., Herr, K., & Nihlen, A. (1994). *Studying your own school: An educator's guide to qualitative practitioner research.* Thousand Oaks, CA: Corwin.

Arter, J., & McTighe, J. (2001). *Scoring rubrics in the classroom. Using performance criteria for assessing and improving student performance.* Thousand Oaks, CA: Corwin.

Banathy, B. (1991). *System design of education: A journey to create the future.* Englewood Cliffs, NJ: Educational Technology Publications.

Bernard, H. R. (2000). *Social research methods.* Thousand Oaks, CA: Sage.

Bernhardt, V. (1998). *The school portfolio: A comprehensive framework for school improvement.* Larchmont, NY: Eye on Education.

Bracey, G. (1997). *Understanding education statistics: It's easier (and more important) than you think.* Arlington, VA: Educational Research Service.

Bransford, J., Brown, A., & Cocking, R. (Eds.). (1999). *How people learn: Brain, mind, experience and school.* Washington, DC: National Academy Press.

Bridges, W. (1991). *Managing transitions: Making the most of change.* New York: Addison-Wesley.

Campbell, D., & Stanley, J. (1966). *Experimental and quasi-experimental designs for research.* Chicago: Rand McNally.

Cox, J. (1996). *Your opinion, please! How to build the best questionnaires in the field of education.* Thousand Oaks, CA: Corwin.

Fowler, F. J., Jr. (1995). *Improving survey questions.* Thousand Oaks, CA: Sage.

Fullan, M. (1993). *Change forces: Probing the depths of educational reform.* Bristol, PA: Falmer.

Fullan, M. (1999). *Change forces: The sequel.* Philadelphia, PA: Falmer.

Fullan, M. (2001). *The new meaning of educational change* (3rd ed.). New York: Teachers College Press.

Gall, M., Borg, W., & Gall, J. (1996). *Educational research: An introduction.* White Plains, NY: Longman.

Gladwell, M. (2000). *The tipping point: How little things can make a big difference.* Boston: Little, Brown.

Glesne, C., & Peshkin, A. (1992). *Becoming qualitative researchers: An introduction.* White Plains, NY: Longman.

Gordon, R. L. (1980). *Interviewing: Strategies, techniques, and tactics* (3rd ed.). Homewood, IL: Dorsey.

Guskey, T. (2000). *Evaluating professional development.* Thousand Oaks, CA: Corwin.

Hall, G., & Hord, S. (1984). *Change in schools: Facilitating the process*. Albany: State University of New York.

Herman, J., & Winters, L. (1992). *Tracking your school's success*. Newbury Park, CA: Corwin.

Hall, G., & Hord, S. (1984). *Change in schools: Facilitating the process*. Albany: State University of New York.

Hatry, H. P., van Houten, T., Plantz, M. C., & Greenway, M. T. (1996). *Measuring program outcomes: A practical approach*. Alexandria, VA: United Way of America.

Herman, J., & Winters, L. (1992). *Tracking your school's success*. Newbury Park, CA: Corwin.

Holcomb, E. (1999). *Getting excited about data: How to combine people, passion and proof*. Thousand Oaks, CA: Corwin.

Jacob, E. (1999). *Cooperative learning in context: An educational innovation in everyday classrooms*. Albany: State University of New York Press.

Katzenback, J. R., & Smith, D. K. (1993). *The wisdom of teams*. New York: HarperCollins.

Killion, J. (2001). *Evaluating the link between staff development and student achievement*. Oxford, OH: National Staff Development Council.

Krueger, R. A., & Casey, M. A. (2000). *Focus groups* (3rd ed.). Thousand Oaks, CA: Sage.

Land, G., & Jarman, B. (1992). *Breakpoint and beyond*. New York: HarperCollins.

The Learning Institute for Nonprofit Organizations. (2000). *Outcome measurement: Are you making a difference?* [Videotape and Facilitators' Guide]. (Excellence in Nonprofit Leadership and Management Enrichment series). Madison, WI: Author.

Lipnack, J., & Stamps, J. (1993). *The teamnet factor*. Essex Junction, VT: Oliver Wight.

Mattessich, P., & Monsey, B. (1992). *Collaboration: What makes it work*. St. Paul, MN: Amherst H. Wilder Foundation.

McKnight, J. (1995). *The careless society: Community and its counterfeits*. New York: Basic Books.

McKnight, J., & Kretzmann, J. (1993). *Building communities from the inside out: A path toward finding and mobilizing a community's assets*. Evanston, IL: Northwestern University, Center for Urban Affairs and Policy Research, Neighborhood Innovations Network.

Mintzberg, H. (1979). *The structuring of organizations*. Englewood Cliffs, NJ: Prentice Hall.

Moore, G. (1991). *Crossing the chasm*. New York: HarperCollins.

National Commission on Teaching and America's Future. (1996). *What matters most: Teaching for America's future*. Available at: http://www.tc.columbia.edu/~teachcomm

Parsons, B. (1998). Using a systems change approach to building communities. In *The policymakers' program: The first five years: Implementation tools* (Vol. 2). St. Louis, MO: The Danforth Foundation.

Parsons, B., & Lupe, C. (2000). *Vision into action: Insights from a change of course*. Boulder, CO: InSites.

Parsons, B. A. (1999, April). *Questions raised by contrasting school-university partnerships with community-university partnerships*. Paper presented at the annual meeting of the American Educational Research Association, Montreal, Canada.

Patton, M. (1997). *Utilization-focused evaluation*. Thousand Oaks, CA: Sage.

Preskill, H., & Torres, R. T. (1999). *Evaluative inquiry for learning in organizations*. Thousand Oaks, CA: Sage.

Preskill, H., & Torres, R. T. (2000). *Readiness for Organization Learning and Evaluation instrument (ROLE)*. Albuquerque, University of New Mexico Press.

Price Waterhouse Change Integration Team. (1995). *Better change*. New York: Irwin.

Reisman, J., & Clegg, J. (2000). *Outcomes for success!* Seattle, WA: The Evaluation Forum.

Rényi, J. (1996). *Teachers take charge of their learning: Transforming professional development for student success*. Washington, DC: The NEA Foundation for the Improvement of Education.

Rogers, E. (1995). *Diffusion of innovations*. New York: Free Press.

Sanders, J. (2000). *Evaluating school programs: An educator's guide*. Thousand Oaks, CA: Corwin.

Schein, E. (1985). *Organizational culture and leadership: A dynamic view*. San Francisco: Jossey-Bass.

Schensul, J. (1999). Mapping social networks, spatial data, and hidden populations. In J. Schensul & M. LeCompte (Eds.), *Ethnographer's toolkit* (Vol. 4). Walnut Creek, CA: AltaMira.

Schensul, J., & LeCompte, M. (Eds.). (1999). *Ethnographer's toolkit*. Walnut Creek, CA: AltaMira.

Senge, P. (1990). *The fifth discipline*. New York: Doubleday/Currency.

Senge, P., Cambron-McCabe, N., Lucas, T., Smith, B., Dutton, J., & Kleiner, A. (2000). *Schools that learn*. New York: Doubleday.

Senge, P., Kleiner, A., Roberts, C., Ross, R., & Smith, B. (1994). *The fifth discipline fieldbook*. New York: Doubleday.

Senge, P., Kleiner, A., Roberts, C., Ross, R., & Smith, B. (1999). *The dance of change*. New York: Doubleday.

Simon, A., & Boyer, E. (1974). *Mirrors for behavior III: An anthology of observation instruments* (3rd ed.). Philadelphia: Research for Better Schools.

Stiggins, R. (1994). *Student-centered classroom assessment*. New York: Macmillan.

Stiggins, R. (2000). *Student-involved classroom assessment*. Upper Saddle River, NJ: Merrill.

Strebel, P. (1992). *Breakpoints: How managers exploit radical business change*. Boston: Harvard Business School Press.

Stufflebeam, D. (2001, Spring). *Evaluation models* (New Directions for Evaluation, Monograph No. 89). San Francisco: Jossey-Bass.

Thomas, S. (1999). *Designing surveys that work!* Thousand Oaks, CA: Corwin.

Torres, R. T., Preskill, H., & Piontek, M. (1996). *Evaluation strategies for communicating and reporting: Enhancing learning in organizations*. Thousand Oaks, CA: Sage.

United Way of America. (1996). *Measuring program outcomes: A practical approach*. Alexandria, VA: Author.

Wheatley, M. J. (2001). *Leadership and the new science*. San Francisco: Berrett-Koehler.

Wiggins, G., & McTighe, J. (1998). *Understanding by design*. Alexandria, VA: Association for Supervision and Curriculum Development.

Worthen, B., Sanders, J., & Fitzpatrick, J. (1997). *Program evaluation: Alternative approaches and practical guidelines*. New York: Longman.

Web Sites

www.cse.ucla.edu (CRESST's Quality School Portfolio)

www.edmin.com (EDmin.Com's Virtual Education)

www.essentialschools.org (The Coalition of Essential Schools)

www.insites.org (InSites)

www.relearning.org (Relearning by Design)

www.assessmentinst.com (The Assessment Institute)

www.wmich.edu/evalctr/ (Western Michigan University Evaluation Center)

www.eval.org (American Evaluation Association)

Name Index

Subject Index

Evaluative Inquiry

*Use this form as a way to stay connected
with new developments, tools, and resources as they emerge.*

Mail this form to:
InSites
Evaluative Inquiry
P.O. Box 1710
Grand Lake, CO 80447

Or you can fill out this form electronically on our Web
site at http://www.insites.org.

Use this form to stay connected with
new developments, tools, and resources related to *Evaluative Inquiry.*

Name _____

Title _____

Organization _____

Type of Organization _____

Address _____

City _____ State/Province _____

Zip/Postal Code _____ Country _____

Is this your home or work address? _____

Phone # _____ Fax # _____

E-mail Address _____

❑ I would like to be informed of new developments and resources for

  evaluative inquiry. I'm particularly interested in _____.

❑ Please inform me about forthcoming publications and seminars.

❑ Here are my comments on *Evaluative Inquiry* (use back of form).

❑ I would like more information about speakers, seminars, consultants, or

  other "in-person" resources on evaluative inquiry.

CORWIN PRESS

The Corwin Press logo—a raven striding across an open book—represents the happy union of courage and learning. We are a professional-level publisher of books and journals for K-12 educators, and we are committed to creating and providing resources that embody these qualities. Corwin's motto is "Success for All Learners."